Haynes

Internet
Genealogy
Manual

© Haynes Publishing 2005

Published by: Haynes Publishing
Sparkford, Yeovil, Somerset BA22 7JJ, UK
Tel: 01963 442030 Fax: 01963 440001
Int. tel: +44 1963 442030 Fax: +44 1963 440001
E-mail: sales@haynes.co.uk
Website: www.haynes.co.uk

British Library Cataloguing in Publication Data:
A catalogue record for this book is available from the British Library

ISBN 1 84425 227 2

Printed in Britain by J. H. Haynes & Co. Ltd., Sparkford

Haynes

Internet Genealogy
Manual

Kyle MacRae

SEMEL ET SE...

Mary Englefield
m. 1697

Thomas Swinburne
b. 2 May 1705

Mary Thornton
nee Meaburne
d. 1 Feb. 1772

Thomas Swinburne
of Pontop Hall
d. Oct. 1825

Charlott...
Spearm...
m. ...

Cristiana
Dillon
m. 1761
d. 15 Aug. 1768

...winburne

Contents

Introduction

If we're absolutely honest about it, family trees are boring. Informative, yes, and a great way of preserving historical records, but basically dull. So we thought we'd do something a little different.

In this book, you'll hear a lot about building a 'family archive'. It sounds as if such a thing goes beyond the confines of a hierarchical list of relatives – but what exactly do we mean by this?

Simply this. We're going to suggest that you gather together as many pieces of your family history as you can and publish everything online in a website. You can then expand this site at will as your family grows or you uncover more facts and heirlooms. As well as merely collecting information, you can create multimedia files that bring a fresh perspective to your family history. The goal is threefold: to bring your family to life, to preserve priceless memories forever, and to share the results with family far and near. You'll end up with a dynamic, living, ever-changing archive that captures and preserves your family history through past, present and future.

Beyond the family tree

The moment you embark on a genealogy project you'll begin to amass all manner of information and paperwork. There's no substitute for hard graft and you simply have to begin with facts, figures, old documents and official records. If you need help with

Root around in the back of wardrobes for family photographs, documents, letters and diaries. If something sheds light on a subject's life, it should be in your family archive website.

Just a few web pages and a video from Grandfather Judd's scrapbook.

conducting such research, consult any of the traditional genealogy books. We can particularly recommend *Ancestral Trails* by Mark Herber, published by Sutton (ISBN 0-7509-3510-3).

But allow us to encourage you to think a little laterally, too. When thinking about any particular family member, ask yourself whether you can lay hands on anything that adds colour and depth. An old snuff box or ring that you can photograph, perhaps? A fragment of a document that's worth scanning? Newspaper clippings, wedding photographs, school details, old

stories…all these and more deserve a place in an archive. If a relative is still alive, wouldn't it be rewarding to capture them on tape or on film reminiscing about the old days? Also think about what you might create yourself to put a life into historical perspective, such as a map of somebody's movements or a timeline that plots their life against significant world events.

Tools for the job

There are various ways to approach such a project but one key facet is dedicated genealogy software that helps you pull together and make sense of your raw genealogy data. We'll use a program called Heritage Family Tree Deluxe that does just this.

One of the appealing things about Heritage Family Tree Deluxe (and other such programs) is its scrapbook feature. This gives you a way of attaching multimedia files to any individual in the family tree. For instance, Grandad's scrapbook could contain a scanned copy of his 'demob' papers, a few photographs and perhaps an audio or video clip.

The other central tool is, of course, the internet. Throughout this book, we'll use the internet in two profitable ways: to research and share genealogical information and to publish a family archive as a fully functioning website. We'll show you some of the best web resources around, and step you through the technicalities of web design at an absolute beginner's level. We'll also show you how to purchase an internet domain name and buy some personal web space.

What we won't do is print a thousand untested web links and leave you to get on with it!

We'll show you how to turn dry names and dates into a multi-faceted family tree and, ultimately, into an online family archive.

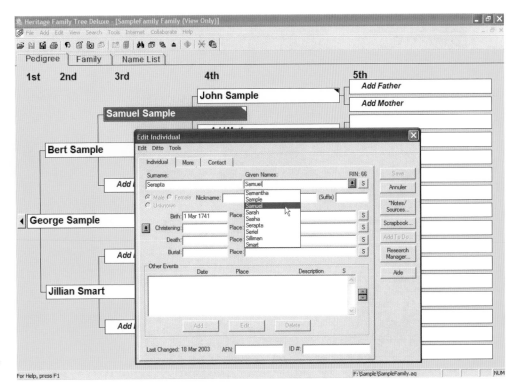

PART **1**

Getting under way

PART

Pen versus PC

A family tree is a visual depiction of you and your family from your ancestors to the present day. It is an important historical record, based on fact but frequently augmented with conjecture. It can give you a sense of belonging, a sense of having roots, a sense of your place in history. It can also be preserved for and expanded by future generations of your family, and is thus a living document.

Above all, a family tree is personal. As we shall see, there are various conventions governing the best way to collate and share your data, but 'data' doesn't really capture what a family tree is all about. Grandad is more than a bunch of dates and Great Uncle Willie deserves more than a distant mention on some outlying branch. This is why we will take the opportunity in this book to go well beyond the usual dry presentation of a family tree and show you how to produce something altogether funkier. After all, this is the digital age; and if the digital age means anything at all, it means unlimited flexibility.

Problems with paper

Every family tree is different from every other. You cannot simply buy a template and fill in the blanks. Basically, you have to get out your ruler and pencil and draw it. That sounds easy enough when you start with yourself and work sideways (brothers and sisters) and upwards one level (parents, aunts and uncles), but by the time you hit the second generation (grandparents and all their kin on both the paternal and the maternal sides of your family), you'll be on your second ream of paper.

Moreover, you'll learn very quickly indeed that you need at least two copies of your fledgling tree: a rough working copy that is subject to near-infinite revisions, and a master copy onto which to transcribe your final findings. Except that once you go back a couple of generations, your findings are seldom final. At best, you are likely to have lots of gaps or unconfirmed dates and names. At worst, some key details will be simply wrong and you'll have to make a full-scale revision (Auntie's memory not being what it was…). You have to constantly check and recheck your work, and it's painstaking, laborious and tedious work.

Which is fine if you don't mind painstaking, laborious, tedious work – but there's another problem. A paper-based family tree quickly becomes an unwieldy document. You inevitably end up having to stick extension papers onto the main tree to fit on newly discovered relatives and their kids, and a tree that started on a page rapidly expands to fill your table and eventually a wall. An alternative approach is to compile lots of little trees that split different strands of your family into self-contained sections, but then there's no way to see how all the family members connect with one another. In other words, you lose the big picture.

But that's not all. Handwriting can be difficult to read and it needs to be small in order to fit all the information onto the tree.

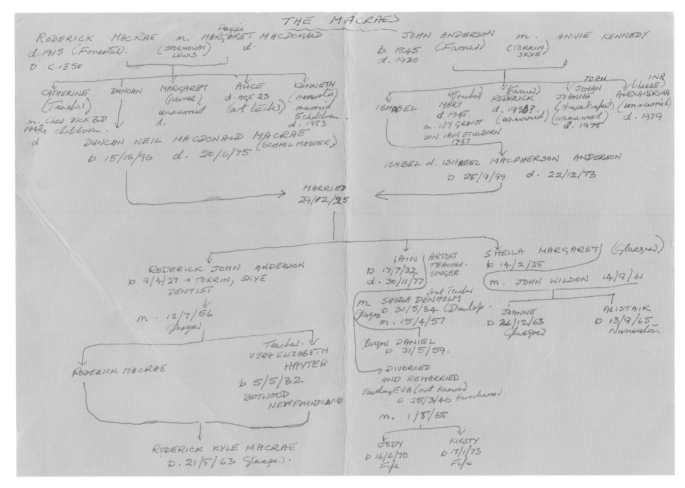

A rough working copy is essential when compiling a family tree. Be prepared to invest heavily in sticky tape, too.

This makes it very hard for family members with poor eyesight to read and enjoy all your hard work. And how are you going to share it with them anyway? If your tree is on paper, at the very least you will need to make photocopies – but how can you do this if you end up with multiple sheets tacked together in all directions?

Still not convinced that paper is the wrong approach? Then consider this. As members of your family get married (or divorced and remarried), you will want to add the new in-laws to your record. The children of these marriages will also want to see the lineage of both parents. This introduces a whole new branch to the tree. Where will you put it? Is there any space left on the wall?

The electronic advantage

If paper is inherently limited in scope and a pain to work with, the obvious alternative is to design and build your family tree on a computer. This has several immediately appealing advantages:

- Your family tree can grow to whatever size you want it to be.
- It is easy to edit so there's no need for a master and working copies.
- Working from just one copy means less chance of making mistakes when transcribing information.
- You can easily add new dates and branches as new people join the family, babies are born, people die, etc.
- You can arrange and view the tree in whatever way you wish,

perhaps focusing on one particular person for while or 'zooming out' to see the bigger picture.

● You can enlarge sections of the tree to cater for poor eyesight.

● You can email the tree in part or in full to other family members and invite them to check your findings and make their own contributions.

● It's easy to reproduce specific parts of the tree to cater for specific relatives.

● You can produce embellished copies, perhaps printed onto luxury paper and framed, to give as gifts.

● You can copy (back up) your work time and time again, thereby ensuring that your work in progress – and a family tree is *always* a work in progress – survives any disaster.

● You can devote more of your time to the interesting part of genealogy – raw research – and less to the dull slog of writing it all down.

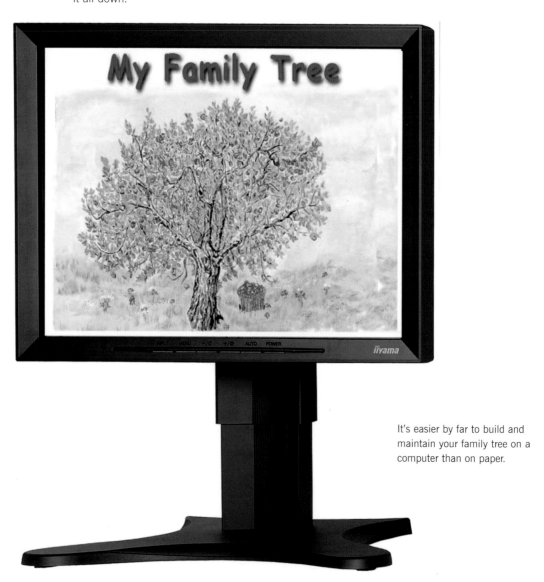

It's easier by far to build and maintain your family tree on a computer than on paper.

Brown, Spray , Phillips and Smith Families

Entries: 1540   **Updated:** 2004-07-11 12:51:01 UTC (Sun)   **Contact:** John Brown

A work in progress: additions and corrections are welcome.

<u>**Index**</u> | <u>**Individual**</u> | <u>**Ahnentafel**</u> | <u>**Download GEDCOM**</u>

<u>Display pedigree in table format</u>

```
                        /_SMITH Christopher (I) b: ca. 1599
        /_SMITH Cristopher (II) b: Jan 1630 d: 1716
        |       |                               /_TOWNLEY Henry
        |       |                       /_TOWNLEY Lawrence II
        |       |               /_TOWNLEY Lawrence III b: abt. 1543 d: Jan 1596
        |       |               |       \_HESKETH Helen
        |       |       /_TOWNLEY Laurence IV b: 1594 d: 1665
        |       |       |       |       /_HARTLEY John
        |       |       |       \_HARTLEY Margaret (Mary?) b: abt. 1574
        |       \_TOWNLEY Elizabeth b: bf. 1599 d: Dec 1679
        |               |       /_HALSTEAD John
        |               \_HALSTEAD Jennete b: ABT 1594 d: 1623
        |                       \_UNKNOWN Elizabeth
   _SMITH John b: AFT 1660
        \_UNKNOWN Elizabeth
```

Share your family history with the world on the web.

Publishing your findings

Once you make the commitment to compiling a computer-based family tree, another unparalleled opportunity suddenly opens up: you can publish your work on the internet. Why would you want to do this?

● Family members around the world can view and share your findings at any time, and it doesn't cost you a penny in paper or postage.

● You can invite your whole family to share in your project, perhaps inviting relatives to email you further information, to correct mistakes and to chat with other members of the family in a private online discussion group (see p47).

● You can make your family history available to other genealogists. You never know, they might even be able to fill in some of your gaps.

Compiling your archive

Finally, consider this. Each and every family has a vast repository of records. We're talking about snapshots in a shoebox, Grandma's memories of the war, poignant trinkets, baby's first shoes. Start rooting around or asking questions and you'll find that this stuff is practically limitless. Almost without exception, these records can be digitized in one form or another. You can scan documents and photographs, record or film interviews, and photograph objects. Anything that can be copied on to a computer can play a part in your family tree.

Preserve your memories with digital photography.

Except that it's not just a family tree any more, is it? What you have now is something much more worthwhile: a multimedia family archive that encompasses, well, just about anything you want to throw at it. If that old ration book meant the world to a member of your family 60-odd years ago, then that ration book deserves a place in your historical family record. How much more rewarding is that than a dry table of dates? How much more does it say about your family than a catalogue of hatches, matches and dispatches? And how much more valuable will it prove to your children and future generations, each of whom can add their own experiences untrammelled by the artificial restrictions of paper and pencil?

Bring old photos back to life by including them in your online family archive.

PART  Understanding family trees

A family tree should always include the following information about anyone contained within it:

- Full name
- Date of birth
- Date of marriage or marriages
- Date of death.

This gathering of purely statistical information, although vital, can be rather dry and uninspiring after a while, but your family tree does not have to stop there. It can become as complex as you wish to make it, depending on what your ultimate goal is.

For instance, you can go on to discover so much more about your ancestors, such as where they were born, where and how they lived, occupations, causes of death, and associated places and events. It all goes together to build a fascinating family history and helps you really get under the skin of your ancestors.

Planning a tree

The traditional image most people have of a family tree is that of a spidery network of lines drawn inside a family bible, with the oldest known family member at the top and new lines added as people married and had children. For the genealogist today, the process works in reverse. You have to trace history backwards, piecing together information as and when you can. The family bible's starting point is your conclusion and is quite possibly unknown to you when you start. But of course your family is still growing so you have to work forwards through time as well. What we need, then, is a flexible family tree that accommodates both new additions to the family and your ancestors as they are

The family bible is the traditional home for family history.

revealed to you. There are numerous possible layouts for such a family tree.

At the simplest level, a family tree is essentially a study of bloodline descent from a particular ancestor or ancestors. Working back through either or both the male and female lines – that is, through your father's and mother's lineages – it details the names, births, marriages and deaths of your parents, grandparents, great-grandparents and even great-great-grandparents, if records can be found. It does not include brothers, sisters or any other relatives.

This kind of tree is often called a 'pedigree' or 'ancestry' chart. It's straightforward to compile, helps you identify gaps in your family history and is always a good starting point. It will also help you to determine which part of your family tree you are most interested in and would like to discover more about.

For a pedigree chart, it is also possible to present the information as a series of concentric circles. The inner circle is yourself, followed by ever-increasing circles divided up into sections as the family members radiate out generation by generation. This ensures that you have enough room to write in all the details about each individual.

An extended family tree is the next logical step. This type of family tree includes other relatives so you will have both the main branch for your direct family line – your pedigree – plus branches for indirect ancestors. This type of tree can become very large very quickly indeed, particularly when you reach the cousin and second-cousin stage, so it is best to break it down into sections, to make it more manageable.

You could also choose to concentrate on one specific aspect of your heritage. For instance, you could focus on:
● All known descendants of a certain ancestor.
● Descendants through one male line (e.g. your father, his father, and his grandfather) and their direct descendants. Tracing the female maternal line is possible but tends to be considerably harder because of the tradition that a wife takes her husband's surname.
● All relatives with the same surname.

When compiling an electronic family tree, these upfront planning issues are secondary because you simply enter each family member's details in any order you like and then view the entire tree in whichever format you prefer.

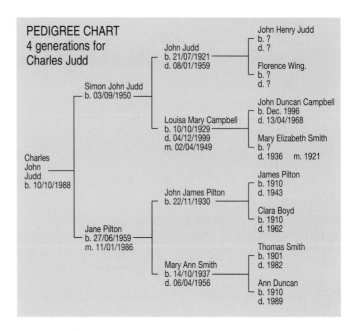

A pedigree chart over four generations for Charles Judd.

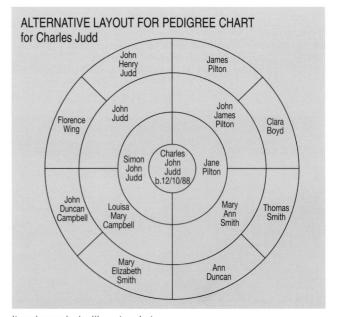

It no longer looks like a tree but this concentric circle approach offers a good deal of flexibility. Here we see Charles John Judd's heritage through four generations.

Conventions

There are some established rules on the way you should enter your information so that it can be understood by anyone. The central principles are these:

- Dates of birth and death are entered below each name.
- Children are arranged in order of their age, eldest first, linked by a line to their parents' marriage.
- People of the same generation (i.e. siblings and cousins) should be positioned at the same level within the tree so that each distinct generation can be seen at a glance.

To make data entry less cumbersome, genealogists have adopted a range of common abbreviations and symbols:

- **b.** means date born
- **bapt.** means date baptised
- **d.** means date died
- **bur.** means date buried
- **m.** or **=** means date married
- the date of a marriage is written under the **=** or under the name of the wife
- multiple spouses are numbered so **= (2)** means second wife and **= (3)** means third wife
- children born out of wedlock are shown by wavy lines
- If you are certain that a marriage produced no children, **no issue** is written below the **=**
- unproven descent is shown by broken lines
- uncertain facts are shown by **?**

Once you have your simple tree – names, births, deaths, marriages – and have decided upon the scope of your records, you can continue to add as much information and detail as you wish. Providing, that is, you adopt the electronic approach to genealogy. This is what really brings your family history alive.

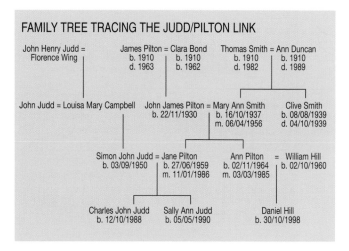

FAMILY TREE TRACING THE JUDD/PILTON LINK

This extended chart shows Charles John Judd's pedigree with a focus on his maternal lineage.

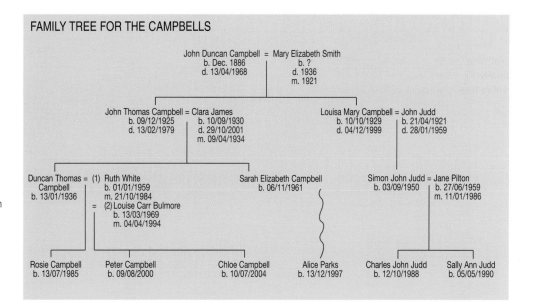

FAMILY TREE FOR THE CAMPBELLS

In this family tree, Mary Elizabeth Smith's birthday is unknown; Duncan Campbell married twice; and Sarah Campbell had a child out of wedlock. These details are indicated by the appropriate symbols.

PART **2** # Internet research

PART 2

Transcriptions versus primary sources

Many genealogy websites have a searchable database. However, the majority of these consist of transcribed information rather than what genealogists call 'primary source' material.

If information is transcribed, it means that somebody somewhere has looked at the primary source material – a census or entries in a church parish register, for example – and copied the information into a database. This is undeniably handy because it means you don't have to do the legwork yourself. However, there is always the possibility that errors have been made in the transcription. Names being spelled incorrectly and dates being recorded incorrectly are commonplace. Before committing anything to stone, as it were, you should always try to verify any transcribed information by seeking out the original document. In other words, by all means use transcribed databases as your starting point but not, if you want to ensure accuracy (so far as is humanly possible), your end point.

You can view some primary source material on the internet. The entire 1901 UK census, for example, can be viewed in its original glory online. What you see when you view a page of the census is a scanned document, not a transcription. More and more material is becoming available online all the time thanks to digital imaging. All of the primary source document websites currently charge fees, so it could save you money to use a free transcription site first and then switch to a fee-based site when you think you have found the right person and need to view an original document.

Let's now have a look at some of the best online resources.

Could your great-grandmother ever have guessed that her family situation would become global public knowledge?

Person Result List

Click on the image icon 🖼 to connect with your family and view the original census image.

Click on the underlined name A Name for easy to read information. You can then find out who else lived with them by viewing others in the household.

If you find the text difficult to read because of its size, click here to find out how to enlarge it.

▶ **Results: 1-10 of 64 Matches**

Census Home Page
Contact Us
Help
FAQs
Site Tour
Research Assist

Search For
Person
  Person Search
Place
  Address Search
  Place Search
  Institution Search
  Vessel Search
View Pages
  Direct Access

Sessions
  What are they?
  Open/Resume
  Suspend/Logout
  My Session
  Print Ordering

Useful Links
National Archives'
email updates

£ Charge

Image	Name	Age	Where Born	Administrative County	Civil Parish	Occupation
🖼	Gertrude Smith	6M	London Bermondsey	London		
🖼	Gertrude Smith	7M	London Carlton St N W	London	St Pancras	
🖼	Gertrude Smith	11M	London Willesen	Kent	Maidstone	
🖼	Gertrude Smith	5	London Battersea	London	Battersea	
🖼	Gertrude Smith	5	London Islington	London	Islington	
🖼	Gertrude Smith	5	London Kensington	London	Kensington	
🖼	Gertrude Smith	5	London Pimlico	Berkshire	New Windsor	
🖼	Gertrude Smith	6	London Battersea	London	Battersea	
🖼	Gertrude Smith	6	London Clapham	London	Clapham	

INTERNET RESEARCH

Essential websites

As we remarked in the introduction, you can use the
internet in two distinct ways: for research and for sharing
your work. In this section, we'll look at some of the
must-see online genealogical resources. One word of
warning, or even a disclaimer: this is very far from being
a complete list! There are thousands of sites out there
that can and do prove fantastic resources for the amateur
historian. The sites we mention specifically are simply
among those that we have found to be the most useful.

You can also do very well indeed, straight off the bat, with a
search engine like Google (**www.google.com**). Enter a couple of
pertinent key words such as your family name plus 'genealogy'
and 'research' and see what you find.

BBC family history
www.bbc.co.uk/history/community/family
This site was originally set up to augment a BBC2 series on
tracing family histories and it gives an excellent introduction to
the subject. It guides you through all the various resources
available to a genealogist with lots of tips and advice on how to
search for your ancestors.

The Bloodlines section contains clickable timelines that let you
explore many different moments in British history, with links to
further information. It covers lots of unusual topics that get little
coverage elsewhere. The page about wartime child emigration, for
example, gives an overview of what happened to children during
World War Two. This background is supported with links to relevant
external sites such as the National Archives website and passenger
lists for ships that took children to Australia and Canada.

Scroll through the timeline and
look for events taking place in
Britain during your ancestors'
lifetimes.

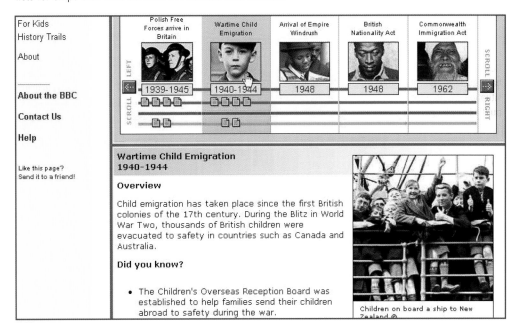

Children on board a ship to New
Zealand ©

Some great tips to help you explore an area of family history that receives little coverage elsewhere.

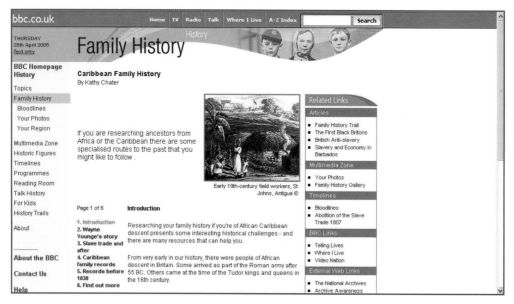

This site is also one of the few online resources to give an overview of Afro-Caribbean family history, together with pointers on how and where to search for further information.

The online photo gallery is particularly useful to anyone trying to date a photograph. You can scroll through hundreds of photographs grouped into numerous categories such as Working Lives, Country Life and Childhood. All of the photos are captioned and dated so, by looking for similarities between your photos and those on the site, you might be able to pinpoint at least the decade and maybe even the year that one of your mysterious photos was taken. You can also submit your photos to the online gallery. The site provides step-by-step instructions on how to do this.

The whole site is written in an easy-to-understand style that avoids a lot of the genealogy jargon – and there really is a *lot* of this – found on other sites so it's very accessible for the novice. The Family History Trail section on how to use the online 1901 census is particularly good and will save you hours of time and frustration when you log into the official census site, as all family historians invariably do sooner or later.

Browse hundreds of photographs and add your own to the collection.

A useful overview of the 1901 census with tips on how to use it.

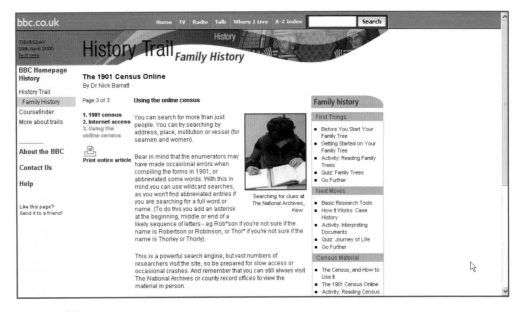

GENUKI

www.genuki.org.uk

GENUKI is an unmissable site for anyone with even a passing interest in researching their family history in the British Isles. It is a virtual reference library of all the primary source material that is currently available to genealogists wanting to research their roots in the UK and Ireland. It's free to use and is maintained by volunteers.

GENUKI has over 45,000 pages so it can, naturally, be a little daunting to navigate at first. Try clicking the 'Guidance for First-Time Users' link on the home page and taking it, slowly, from there.

The large and continually growing information section includes an excellent guide for people new to genealogy. This can be accessed from the home page by clicking on the 'Getting started in genealogy' link.

The bulk of the site comprises comprehensive lists of links to other sites, all indexed and searchable right down through county

Click here to find out just what this enormous site contains.

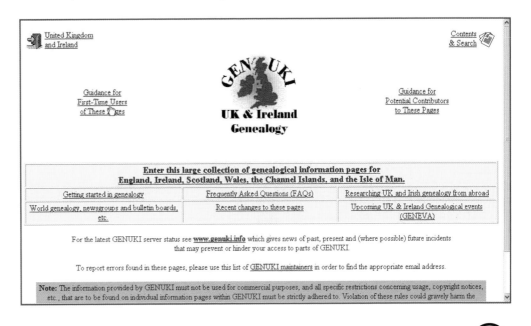

to parish level. Click the 'United Kingdom and Ireland' link in the top-left corner of the home page to visit the regional pages. Here you will find a clickable map of the British Isles. Select first the country and then the county you are interested in.

On each county page, you will find a comprehensive range of clickable links covering a wide range of research categories, including local history societies, church and military records, local newspapers, orphanages, voting registers, maps and cemeteries.

Any of these categories will take you to a wealth of local information, often with incredible attention to detail. Here, for instance, the military history category for Buckinghamshire

You'll probably spend most of your time browsing the regional pages of the GENUKI site.

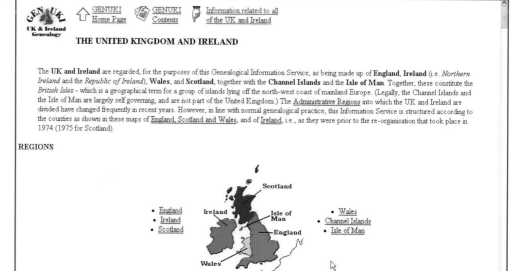

No shortage of links. In this case, we're looking at Buckinghamshire.

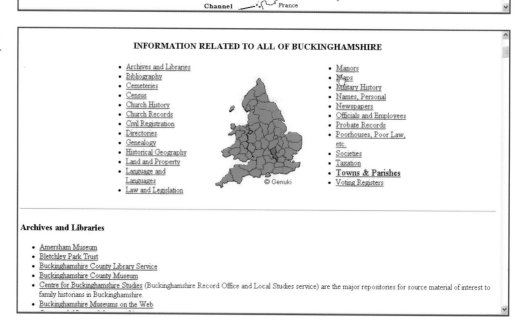

includes a clickable photograph of the Boer War Memorial in Aylesbury, the county town.

The site's excellent search facility allows you to search not only the GENUKI site but also the websites of the National Archives, the Society of Genealogists, the Federation of Family History Societies and the Guild of One-Name Studies. Just enter a place name, a surname, the name of a church or school, a local newspaper or an occupation. There is a good chance that it will appear somewhere on one of these sites.

For example, a search for the village of Haddenham returns 102 results, all of which are relevant leads and any one of which could uncover vital information for your quest.

By zooming in on this image, it is possible to read the names on the memorial.

Smart searching made simple.

All names in blue in the diagram above are active hyper-links.

It should be noted that at each level in the hierarchy, information is arranged under the same alphabetically-ordered set of topic headings, e.g. Biography, Census, Church Records, Description & Travel, History, Maps, Probate Records, etc. For further guidance see "How this information Service is Organised", and for a full list of possible topic headings see How the information on this server is presented to the user.

GENUKI Search Engine

If you are having difficulty finding the information you require, the **GENUKI Search Engine** lets you search the contents of **ALL GENUKI pages** plus the PRO, SoG, FFHS and GOONS web sites. It also includes all the Family History Society and County Surname Interest List sites linked from GENUKI.

haddenham   Search

GENUKI Gazetteer

If you need to to find a place in the *United Kingdom* or determine which of our pages contain information about it, then try searching in the GENUKI Gazetteer.

Haddenham   Find place

Surname lists

There are a large number of listings of the surnames being researched by various Internet users. Details can be found in the listing of all the Surname Lists available. and also under the heading "Genealogy" on the appropriate county pages.

E-mail lists

A number of e-mail lists exist covering various parts of the country. If your research interests cover one of these areas, then joining the appropriate list would be

FreeGEN

http://freeukgen.rootsweb.com

This is an initiative to make more primary source material available online, completely free of charge. It has been set up by GENUKI in direct response to the growing number of commercial sites charging fees to access the same information.

Volunteers are recruited to transcribe or scan original documents and primary source materials that currently only exist in paper, microfilm or CD-ROM formats.

There are currently three FreeGEN projects underway: FreeBMD, FreeREG and FreeCEN.

1. FreeBMD www.freebmd.org.uk

This is an ongoing project to transcribe the Civil Registration index of births, marriages and deaths for England and Wales, and to provide free internet access to the transcribed records. The records begin in 1837.

Search results appear in list format, giving the name, month, year of birth and location. The red Info button is not as useful as

Delve deep into Civil Registration records courtesy of FreeBMD.

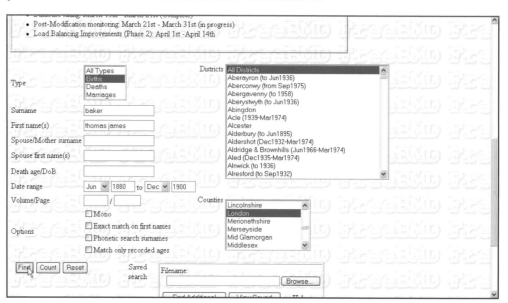

Click a place name for further information about an area where an ancestor once lived. This can all be added to your family archive later.

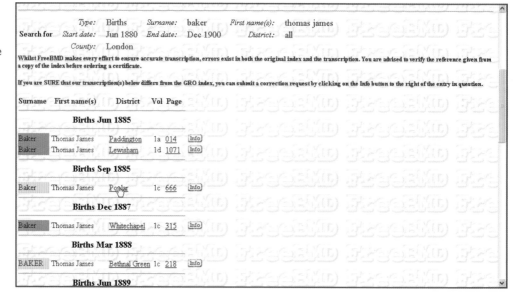

you may think, however – all it tells you is the name of the person who transcribed that particular entry.

To determine whether an individual is really your missing ancestor, you should order a copy of the original certificate from which the information has been transcribed. In many cases, it is not possible to view the actual documents online.

The cheapest way to do this is through the General Register Office (GRO) website at **www.gro.gov.uk/gro/content/research/ obtainingcertificates/certificatefees.asp**. Use the GRO reference number provided by the FreeBMD search to order the appropriate document. However, each certificate costs £7 so this could prove a costly exercise if you are unsure about exact dates or names.

The General Register Office site also has a useful family history section detailing the types of certificates on record that might be of interest to a genealogist.

2. FreeREG www.freereg.org.uk

This will operate in a similar way to the freeBMD site, providing free internet searches of baptism, marriage and burial records. These are currently being transcribed from parish and non-conformist church registers in the UK. It is not yet possible to conduct a search as the data is still being compiled and collated, but it's worth bookmarking and revisiting from time to time to check on progress.

3. FreeCEN www.freecen.org.uk

This branch of the FreeGEN initiative will provide a free-to-view online searchable database of the 19th century UK census returns. It has the same easy-to-use search engine as FreeBMD but very few parts of the UK have yet been transcribed.

Indeed, the information held on each of these FreeGEN sites is nowhere near comprehensive, but it is growing day by day. They are all worth a look and you just might find that the part of the country you are interested in has already been covered.

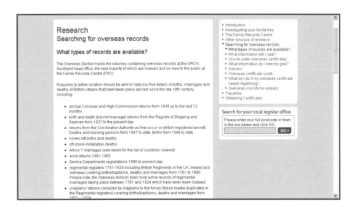

The General register Office provides guidance on what certificates they hold and how to order them.

The GRO website can also advise you about how to search for overseas records of British citizens.

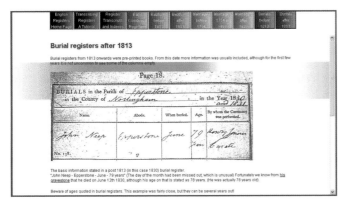

FreeREG shows you examples of actual records to help explain how information is recorded. This is a burial document.

Census transcription is far from complete on FreeCEN but you can check progress on the site.

On the Available Databases page, click on a county to see what information is currently available.

Federation of Family History Societies
www.familyhistoryonline.net

The Federation of Family History Societies is making census data available online on a pay-per-view basis. Local Family History societies across England and Wales have been transcribing various local records, and they are listed here by county. Under Buckinghamshire, for example, it is possible to search through 167,095 entries from the 1851 census and 80,011 entries from the National Burial Index, all carefully transcribed by the Buckinghamshire Family History Society.

When you register and sign into the site, you can conduct free surname searches on any database. If you get a result, you can then click to see further information. If the information has been transcribed from a census, you can click to find out who else was living with that person at that time.

You can view census information in a table, which is so much easier to read than the original document.

If you then want to see fuller information on any of your searches, a charge is sometimes applied. However, all surplus income after costs have been covered is passed on to the Family History Society that transcribed the information you access. Index entries cost 5p and transcriptions cost 7p (except for census entries from 1851 onwards and marriage entries from July 1837 onwards, which both cost 9p).

This individual had seven other people living with him in the same household. Could they all be long lost relatives?

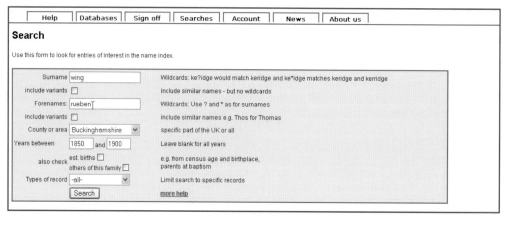

This household information is just as it would have appeared in the census but it is presented in an easy-to-read table.

Entry	Forenames	Surname	Relationship	Condition	Gender	Age	Occupation	Birthplace	Address	Town	County	Country	Class	Piece	Folio	Page	FHL_film	Cost
1	Robert	WING	Head	M	M	49	Ag Lab	Marlow, Buckingham, England	Marlow Common	Great Marlow	Buckingham	England	RG11	1466	110	39	1341355	£0.00
2	Charlotte P.	WING	Wife	M	F	48		Marlow, Buckingham, England	Marlow Common	Great Marlow	Buckingham	England	RG11	1466	110	39	1341355	£0.00
3	Robert	WING	Son	U	M	16	Ag Lab	Marlow, Buckingham, England	Marlow Common	Great Marlow	Buckingham	England	RG11	1466	110	39	1341355	£0.00
4	Henry	WING	Son	U	M	1	Scholar	Marlow, Buckingham, England	Marlow Common	Great Marlow	Buckingham	England	RG11	1466	110	39	1341355	£0.00
5	Rose	WING	Daur	U	F	9	Scholar	Marlow, Buckingham, England	Marlow Common	Great Marlow	Buckingham	England	RG11	1466	110	39	1341355	£0.00
6	Mary A.	WING	Daur	U	F	5	Scholar	Marlow, Buckingham, England	Marlow Common	Great Marlow	Buckingham	England	RG11	1466	110	39	1341355	£0.00
7	Reuben	WING	Son	U	M	4	Scholar	Marlow, Buckingham, England	Marlow Common	Great Marlow	Buckingham	England	RG11	1466	110	39	1341355	£0.00

The Origins Network
www.originsnetwork.com

This is a commercial site with a comprehensive online collection of British and Irish records, dating as far back as the 13th century in some cases. A wide variety of online, searchable information can be found here, including parts of the England & Wales censuses of 1841 and 1871, Marriage and Wills Records, Apprenticeship Records, and Militia Records. There are also maps, plans and galleries of old photographs. A number of indexes compiled by the Society of Genealogists are also available to view, exclusively, through this site.

This site is especially useful to people searching for Irish ancestors, as there is very little Irish genealogical information currently available online. For example, you will find ship passenger lists from 1890 that contain the names, occupations, ages and marital status of over 45,000 Irish people who sailed from Ireland to the USA.

The site also hosts a discussion group, an online shop and a monthly newsletter. The cost of access to both the British and Irish databases is £7.50 for 72 hours; £10.50 per month; £18.50 per quarter; or £34.50 per year. Annual access to just one database is £22.50.

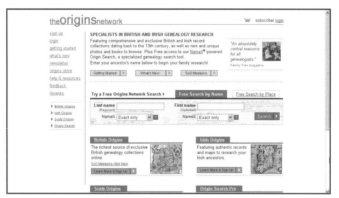

Before subscribing, you can search on a surname for free to see if records are available.

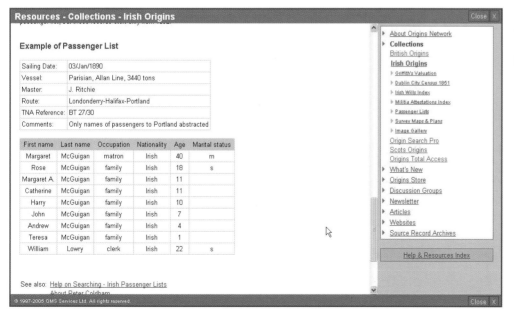

Here we can see passengers who travelled on the ship *Parisian* from Londonderry to Portland, Oregon, in 1890.

Example of Passenger List

Sailing Date:	03/Jan/1890
Vessel:	Parisian, Allan Line, 3440 tons
Master:	J. Ritchie
Route:	Londonderry-Halifax-Portland
TNA Reference:	BT 27/30
Comments:	Only names of passengers to Portland abstracted

First name	Last name	Occupation	Nationality	Age	Marital status
Margaret	McGuigan	matron	Irish	40	m
Rose	McGuigan	family	Irish	18	s
Margaret A.	McGuigan	family	Irish	11	
Catherine	McGuigan	family	Irish	11	
Harry	McGuigan	family	Irish	10	
John	McGuigan	family	Irish	7	
Andrew	McGuigan	family	Irish	4	
Teresa	McGuigan	family	Irish	1	
William	Lowry	clerk	Irish	22	s

See also: Help on Searching - Irish Passenger Lists
About Peter Coldham

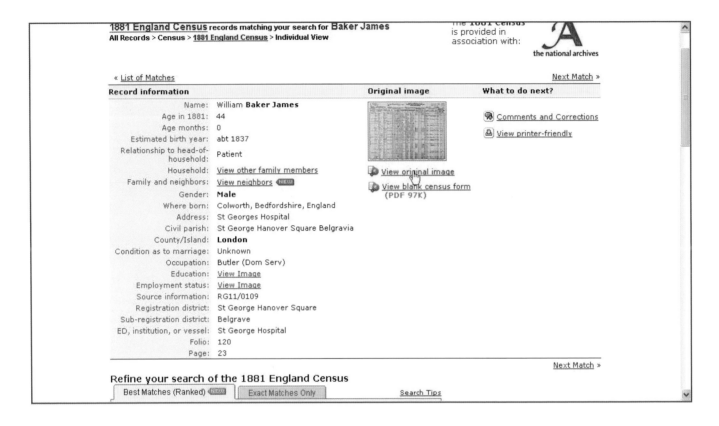

Ancestry.co.uk

www.ancestry.co.uk

This is the commercial arm of RootsWeb, a site where genealogy researchers share research and ask for help. More on RootsWeb on p171.

Ancestry.co.uk holds the following searchable databases:
- 1861–1901 Censuses for England and Wales.
- UK and Ireland Parish and Probate Records. These include 15 million birth, marriage, death, probate, and burial names from historical parish registers in England, Wales, Scotland and Ireland ranging from 1538 to 1837.
- England and Wales Civil Registration Birth, Marriage and Death Indexes. This is a collection of 62 million registered births, marriages and deaths in England and Wales between 1837 and 1983.
- Pallot Marriage Index. A collection of more than 1.7 million marriage entries from England and Wales. Original images of the records are also available.
- Irish Immigrants: New York Port Arrival Records. An index of 600,000 Irish immigrants to the USA between 1846 and 1851.

Ancestry.co.uk charges for access as follows:
- Annual subscription: £69.95
- Quarterly subscription: £29.95
- Pay-per-view: £6.99 (You can view up to 20 premium record pages from any subscriber area for 7 days).

When you undertake a search of a census database, you have the option to view the primary source material.

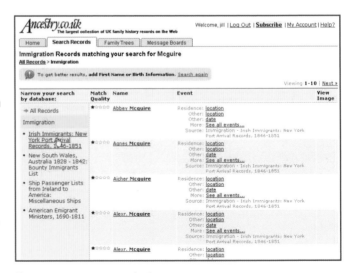

You can narrow your search at each step to home in on particular ancestors.

National Archives

www.nationalarchives.gov.uk

The National Archives is one of the largest archival collections in the world, going back 1,000 years to the Domesday Book. Its website lists catalogues of archives created by individuals, families and a wide range of organisations such as local government bodies, courts, businesses, charities and local societies. These archives are held in hundreds of record offices and other repositories all over the UK.

You cannot view the content of the majority of these archives online; a visit to the National Archives in London is necessary for that. However, the website does have some documents available. Browsing is free but to download a digital image costs £3.50.

The online documents are:

- World War One Campaign Medals. This archive contains over 5 million WWI medal index cards for the British Army and Royal Flying Corps, searchable by name, date, rank and division.
- World War Two Seaman's Medals. Records of medals issued to over 100,000 merchant seamen between 1946 and 2002, searchable by name.
- Wills. Over 1 million wills belonging to relatively wealthy individuals living mainly in the south of England or Wales between 1384 and 1858. It is searchable by name, place and occupation. Original wills of famous people such as William Shakespeare, Oliver Cromwell and Christopher Wren can be viewed online.

In addition to these, the National Archives has linked up with the commercial site Ancestry.co.uk to make the England and Wales censuses from 1971 to 1901 available online (for a fee).

Check the Documents Online page to see what's available over the internet. You have to pay to view the documents.

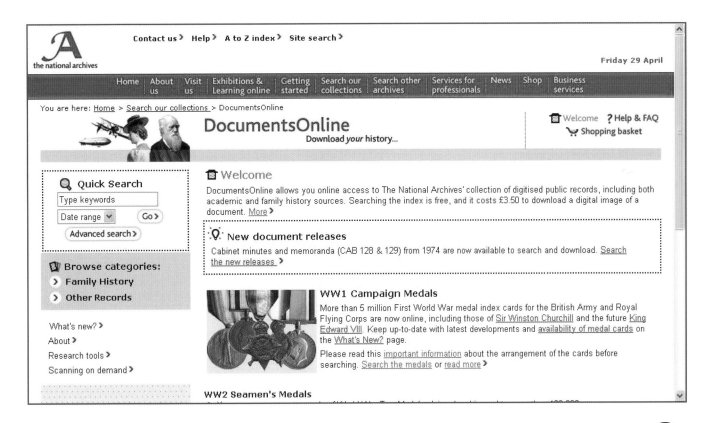

LDS Family Search

www.familysearch.org

One of the beliefs held by members of the Church of Jesus Christ of Latter-Day Saints (LDS) is that they have duties to perform on behalf of their ancestors. To aid them in this, the LDS Church has filmed and indexed baptism and marriage records from the USA and other countries to create the largest, free-to-use genealogical database in the world.

The majority of the names are from records of people who lived between 1500 and 1885, and it includes dates and places of births, christenings, marriages, and other events. The LDS Church has made some of this information available online:

- The 1881 British Census (excluding the data for Scotland)
- The 1881 Canadian Census
- The 1880 US Census
- The Vital Records Index for Denmark, Finland, Mexico, Norway and Sweden
- The US Social Security Death Index.

The site also hosts a huge collection of private websites containing family histories using the GEDCOM system. These are all searchable, making it possible to track down families who share the same name and even the same ancestors as you.

For more on GEDCOM, see Part 8.

You will find some useful features on the home page to help get you started.

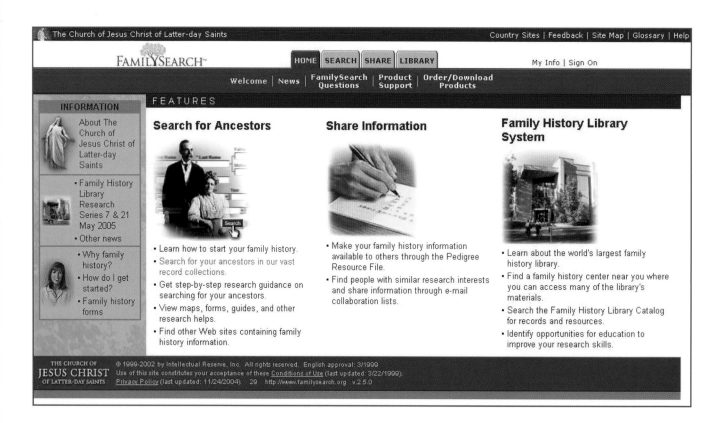

PART  **Census records of the UK**

This is a record of every individual living in every property in the United Kingdom on one particular day. There has been a census taken every ten years since 1801, although people's names were not recorded until 1841. Unfortunately, the census of 1931 was destroyed during World War Two and there was no census taken in 1941 because the country was at war.

Invaluable information

A census tells you the full name, age and marital status of every person within a household. You will also find their relationship to the head of the household, their gender and their occupation, as well as their parish and county of birth. This makes a census an extremely useful document for tracing family histories. If you have one known family member, you can trace them in the census and find out where they were living, and with whom, at that time. This can often reveal children that you were not previously aware of. Alternatively, if you have an address, you can search on that to find out who was living there at the time of the census.

The general public only has access to a census one hundred years after the event and family historians eagerly await each release. The next census to become available to the public will be the 1911 census, which will be published in January 2012.

Local censuses from as far apart as Cornwall and Fife have been carefully transcribed by family history enthusiasts.

UK CENSUS ONLINE

The information on these pages is for genealogy research only. It may be linked to but not copied in any form without the owners permission

Please note that all these links are not necessarily complete transcripts of the census, many are individual family names.
Use the Search Engine on the Index page to do a quick search of the Towns. But Note it does not search the links Just the names on these pages

Cornish Online Census Project	1851 CENSUSES OF GLOUCESTERSHIRE & SOUTHERN WARWICKSHIRE (Stratford on Avon and Southwards)	Whole Parish of Lambourne, Essex for the year 1841
1851 Co. Antrim Census Ireland	CENSUSES OF SOMERSET	WILTSHIRE CENSUS 1851
NORTHUMBERLAND Index to 1851 Census of Registration District 552, Newcastle St. Andrew's	FIFE 1851 Census (Partial)	FIFE born Strays found on the 1851 Census in England
UPPINGHAM 1851 Census	LLANFAIR 1851 Census	HOLYHEAD 1851 Census
GLAPTHORN Northamptonshire, England 1851 CENSUS	HAMPSHIRE 1851 Census Records	WILTS 1851 Census Surnames
BERKSHIRE UK Surnames appearing in the 1851 Census Returns	Tilney All Saints, Norfolk. 1851 Census	Wigtownshire Parishes Census of 1851
Wirksworth Area CENSUS 1841, 1851, 1861, 1871 and 1881	Papa Westray Census 1851	The Woodchester Census. 1851
BADSEY & ALDINGTON 1841, 1851, 1861, 1871, 1881, 1891, 1901. Kelly's Directory for 1912.	IRELAND Excerpts from A Collection of 1851 Census Records	1851 Census for St. Stephen Brannel, Cornwall, England.
Derbyshire Census Extracts 1851-1881	1851 Census extracts	1851 Census at St. Erth
1851 census return for a workhouse. It lists all the people who were in		Dumfriesshire Census 1851

FreeCEN (see table below) is looking for volunteers to help make census records from 1841-1891 freely available on the internet.

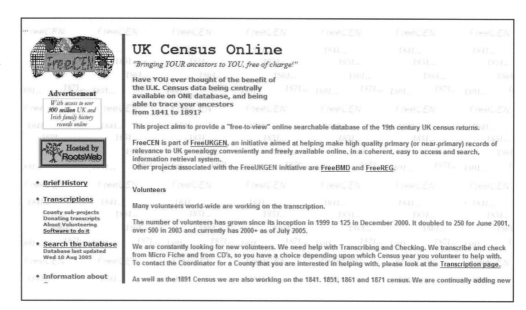

The release of the 1901 census was more exciting than most because it was the first census to be available via the internet. Original census returns were scanned and could be viewed online, with all the information contained within them made fully searchable. True, census information could be found on the internet prior to this through commercial sites and local history sites, but the information had been transcribed so researchers could never be 100% sure that information was accurate. Mistakes could easily have been made, particularly because abbreviations were common practice and all censuses were handwritten in the 19th and early 20th centuries.

For a comprehensive list of transcribed British censuses go to:

http://nzgenealogy.rootschat.net/ukcensus.html

Here you will find links to all kinds of census information. Someone somewhere might just have transcribed an older census taken in the village or town where one of your ancestors lived.

The following table details where you can view census returns for the British Isles online. It indicates whether the information has been transcribed or whether it is possible to view digital images of the primary source material.

	Website Address	Census year(s)	Primary source/ transcribed	Cost
England & Wales	**www.census.pro.gov.uk**	1901	Primary source	Pay to view
England & Wales	**www.familysearch.org**	1881	Transcribed	Free
England & Wales	**www.freecen.org.uk**	1881	Transcribed	Free but site still under construction
England & Wales	**www.ancestry.co.uk**	1861–1901	Primary source/transcribed	Pay to view
England & Wales	**www.britishorigins.com**	1841, 1871	Primary source/transcribed but records not complete	Pay to view
Scotland	**www.scotlandspeople.gov.uk**	1871, 1891 and 1901	Primary source	Pay to view
Scotland	**www.scotlandspeople.gov.uk**	1881	Transcribed	Pay to view
Scotland	**www.scotlandspeople.gov.uk**	1841,1851, 1861	Primary source	Pay to view (due in winter 2005)
Ireland	**www.irishorigins.com**	Dublin City 1851 census	Transcribed	Pay to view

The 1901 Census for England & Wales

www.census.pro.gov.uk

The 1901 census service is now available 24 hours a day, 7 days a week as a full internet service. The information you can find there is as follows:

- Road or street
- Town or village
- Number or name of house
- Whether the house was inhabited or not
- Full name of each person living there
- Relationship to head of family
- Condition as to marriage
- Age last birthday
- Profession or occupation
- Whether employed or not
- Where born
- Whether deaf, dumb, blind, lunatic, imbecile or feeble-minded
- Crews of vessels
- Residents of institutions.

That's quite some compilation. What we need here is a worked example of how to extract useful information from the 1901 census.

From the home page at **www.census.pro.gov.uk**, *you can choose to search for a person or a place. We will search for a person, so select Person Search in the left hand column.*

This will take you to the search fields where you should enter as much information as you can.

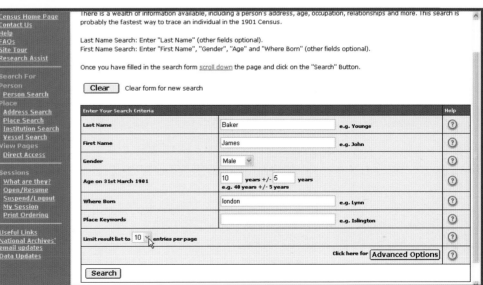

You will now see a list of possible matches, with information on each person's age, place of birth, county, civil parish and occupation.

Person Result List

Click on the image icon to connect with your family and view the original census image.

Click on the underlined name A Name for easy to read information. You can then find out who else lived with them by viewing others in the household.

If you find the text difficult to read because of its size, click here to find out how to enlarge it.

▶ Results: 1-10 of 40 Matches

Image	Name	Age	Where Born	Administrative County	Civil Parish	Occupation
	James Baker	5	London Balham	London	Streatham	
	James Baker	5	London Islington	London	Shoreditch	
	James Baker	5	London Mile End	London	Mile End Old Town	
	James Baker	5	London Poplar	London	Poplar	
	James Baker	5	London West Hampstead	London	Hampstead	
	James Baker	6	London Fulham	London	Fulham	
	James Baker	6	London Shepherds Broh	London	Paddington	
	James Baker	6	London St Giles	London	Islington	
	James Baker	6	London Walworth	London	Nevington	
	James Baker	7	London Camberwell	London	Camberwell	

Next >>

If you have too many results and cannot determine which one you want, try using the Advanced Search. To do this, click to go back to the search fields form and then select Advanced Options at the bottom right of the form.

Last Name Search: Enter "Last Name" (other fields optional).
First Name Search: Enter "First Name", "Gender", "Age" and "Where Born" (other fields optional).

Once you have filled in the search form scroll down the page and click on the "Search" Button.

Clear   Clear form for new search

Enter Your Search Criteria		Help
Last Name	Baker e.g. Youngs	?
First Name	James e.g. John	?
Gender	Male	?
Age on 31st March 1901	10 years +/- 5 years e.g. 40 years +/- 5 years	?
Where Born	london e.g. Lynn	?
Place Keywords	e.g. Islington	?
Limit result list to 10 entries per page		?
	Click here for Advanced Options	?

Search

You will now have new search fields available to you where you can add additional information such as a middle name or occupation.

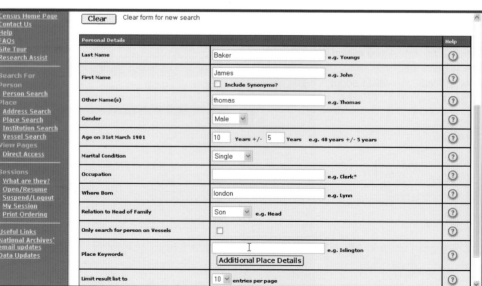

Clear   Clear form for new search

Personal Details		Help
Last Name	Baker e.g. Youngs	?
First Name	James e.g. John ☐ Include Synonyms?	?
Other Name(s)	thomas e.g. Thomas	?
Gender	Male	?
Age on 31st March 1901	10 Years +/- 5 Years e.g. 40 years +/- 5 years	?
Marital Condition	Single	?
Occupation	e.g. Clerk*	?
Where Born	london e.g. Lynn	?
Relation to Head of Family	Son e.g. Head	?
Only search for person on Vessels	☐	?
Place Keywords	e.g. Islington Additional Place Details	?
Limit result list to	10 entries per page	?

Once you have located an individual of interest, you can view transcribed information about that individual by clicking the name. Alternatively, or additionally, you can see the relevant census page by clicking the icon to the left of the name.

Census Home Page
Contact Us
Help
FAQs
Site Tour
Research Assist

Search For
Person
  Person Search
Place
  Address Search
  Place Search
  Institution Search
  Vessel Search
View Pages
  Direct Access

Sessions
  What are they?
  Open/Resume
  Suspend/Logout
  My Session
  Print Ordering

Useful Links
National Archives'
email updates
Data Updates

Image	Name	Age	Where Born	Administrative County	Civil Parish	Occupation
	James Baker	5	London Balham	London	Streatham	
	James Baker	5	London Islington	London	Shoreditch	
	James Baker	5	London Mile End	London	Mile End Old Town	
	James Baker	5	London Poplar	London	Poplar	
	James Baker	5	London West Hampstead	London	Hampstead	
	James Baker	6	London Fulham	London	Fulham	
	James Baker	6	London Shepherds Broh	London	Paddington	
	James Baker	6	London St Giles	London	Islington	
	James Baker	6	London Walworth	London	Newington	
	James Baker	7	London Camberwell	London	Camberwell	

Next >>

To find out how much you have spent, click on 'My Session' Your Session ID is : 6305964

Found it? You can...

- View the image of the original document by clicking on the image icon  to the left of the person's name. **There is a charge for this.**
- View the full transcription details by clicking on the underlined name A Name. **There is a charge for this.**

Netscape users - for help on printing this page click here.

Not found it?

There is a small charge for all of these actions. If this is your first visit, you will be prompted to register and pay online when you click a name in the census. Click the Open button to proceed. There is a minimum charge of £5, which covers a session over seven days. During each session you will be charged 50p for every transcription that you view and 75p for every digital image of the census.

Census Home Page
Contact Us
Help
FAQs
Site Tour
Research Assist

Search For
Person
  Person Search
Place
  Address Search
  Place Search
  Institution Search
  Vessel Search
View Pages
  Direct Access

Sessions
  What are they?
  Open/Resume
  Suspend/Logout
  My Session
  Print Ordering

Useful Links
National Archives'
email updates
Data Updates

Opening or Resuming a Session

You have requested a chargeable Service.

To use the chargeable services, such as View an Image or Person Details, you will need to Open a session. Searches are free, to return to the searches click here.
  What are sessions ?
  What does it cost ?
  How can I pay ?

What to do now ?

Open — You will be able to choose whether to pay by credit/debit card or by using a voucher.
Resume — a credit/debit card session over a secure connection.
Resume — a voucher session over a secure connection.
☐ tick this box if you do NOT wish to use the secure (SSL) connection - **we do not recommend this.**
No Active Session

Payment made, you'll be returned to where you left off. Here we can see the transcribed information about our subject, James J Baker.

Census Home Page
Contact Us
Help
FAQs
Site Tour
Research Assist

Search For
Person
  Person Search
Place
  Address Search
  Place Search
  Institution Search
  Vessel Search
View Pages
  Direct Access

Sessions
  What are they?
  Open/Resume
  Suspend/Logout
  My Session
  Print Ordering

Useful Links
National Archives'
email updates
Data Updates

Person Details

Full Transcription Details for **James J Baker**   View Image/Other Household members   Back to Search Results

National Archives Reference				Schedule Number	
RG Number, Series	Piece	Folio	Page		
RG13	352	106	25	173	

Name		Language
James J Baker		
Relation to Head of Family	Condition as to Marriage	Age Last Birthday	Sex
Son	S	5	M
Profession or Occupation	Employment Status	Infirmity
	Undefined	
Where Born	Address	
London Poplar	1 Prospect Pl	
Civil Parish	Rural District	
Poplar		
Town or Village or Hamlet	Parliamentary Borough or Division	
	Poplar	
Ecclesiastical Parish	Administrative County	
St Matthias	London	
County Borough, Municipal Borough or Urban District	Ward of Municipal Borough or Urban District	

To find out how much you have spent, click on 'My Session' Your Session ID is : 6305964

To see the digital image of the actual census page, click the icon to the left of the name. You will be asked to choose what file format you wish to use. We recommend PDF, for which you will need the free Adobe Reader program. If it's not already on your computer, you can download it from here: **www.adobe.com/ products/acrobat**.

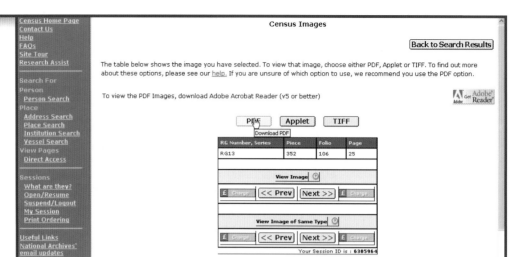

You now need to select to save the file onto your computer. It's worthwhile setting up a special Genealogy folder to keep track of this and other downloads. We'll soon be filling your folder with all sorts of bits and bobs...

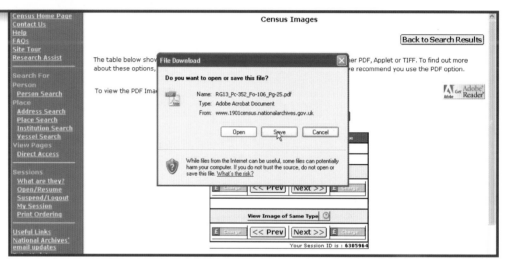

Open the saved PDF file to view it in Adobe Reader. You're now looking at a scanned copy of the original census. The text is often difficult to read so use the zoom tool. Somewhere on this page, you'll find your subject. You might now print this page for your records but you can also include it in your family archive website in the relevant scrapbook (see p150).

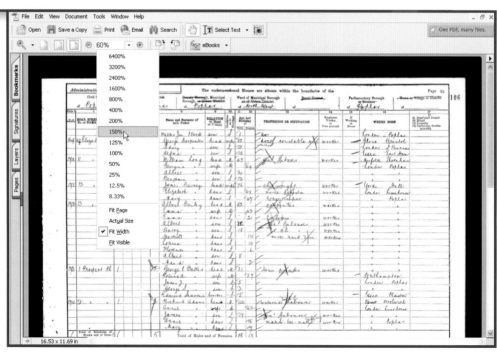

From this page of the 1901 Census, we can tell a good deal about James J Baker:
- His address: 1 Prospect Place, Poplar
- His age: 5 years
- His family situation: father George, aged 31, worked as a house painter; mother Rosinna, aged 27; brother George, aged 2; and Edward Scarces, a boarder, also aged 5. Everyone in the family was born in Poplar except Rosinna, who was born in Southampton. The child boarder was born in Plaistow, Essex.

We also have lots of leads to follow up:
- Now that we know the ages and places of birth for the family members, we could look for their birth certificates.
- We could look for a marriage certificate for George and Rosinna.
- We could find out more about the trade of house painting in the 1900s. Were there any trades guilds to which George might have belonged?
- We could find out why children were boarded. Could Edward be an orphan?
- We could check the 1881 census to see who was living at this address then.

1891 and 1901 Censuses of Scotland

www.scotlandspeople.gov.uk/

ScotlandsPeople is the official online source of parish register, civil registration and census records for Scotland. Containing nearly 40 million records, the database is one of the world's largest resources of genealogical information and one of the largest single information resources on the web. It has a fully searchable index of Scottish births from 1553 to 1904, marriages from 1553 to 1929, and deaths from 1855 to 1954.

You have to register before you can enter the site. You will then be able to select which of the databases you want to look at. The beauty of this site is that you get to search through a very comprehensive list of databases and can view primary source material so, for anyone researching Scottish roots, it really is a must.

When you are ready to begin your search, you are asked to make a payment. The minimum amount is £6 and you can pay online with a credit card. Searching itself is free; you only pay to view an entry. For instance, if your search brings up several pages of names and you want to scroll through them all, it costs one credit per page. If you then want to select one of the names to see further information, that costs five credits. You get 30 credits for your £6 so it doesn't take long to spend them.

Previous searches and downloaded images can be accessed without further charge simply by logging back in to the site in the future. If you wish to order an official, legally admissible copy of

A long list of databases are available once you register

General Register Office for SCOTLAND

www.scotlandspeople.gov.uk

Welcome to the official government source of genealogical data for Scotland

Previous Visit: 29-Apr-2005 13:08
You have no credits

Logged in as: Jill MacRae   Credits Remaining: 0   Buy More Credits

- Home Page
- Search Records
- Shopping Basket
- Previous Searches
- Viewed Images
- Timeline
- Your Details
- Log Out
- About this Site
- What's New
- Features
- Discussion Group
- FAQs
- Help & Other Resources
- Contact Us

You are here: Home Page | Search the Records

Search the Records

Registered Users Only

Choose from one of the index searches below. Help Assistants are available for each of the searches; if you'd like to read more about the searches before you start, please visit our "Help and Other Resources" section, or to read more about tracing your family history, read our Getting Started guide in our Features section.

▶▶▶ **Search Census (1881)**

▶▶▶ **Search Census (1871, 1891, 1901)**

▶▶▶ **Search Old Parish Register (OPR) Births/Christenings (1553-1854)**

▶▶▶ **Search Statutory Register (SR) Births (1855-1904)**

▶▶▶ **Search Old Parish Register (OPR) Marriages/Banns (1553-1854)**

▶▶▶ **Search Statutory Register (SR) Marriages (1855-1929)**

▶▶▶ **Search Statutory Register (SR) Deaths (1855-1954)**

▶▶▶ **Search All Statutory Records**

▶▶▶ **Search All Old Parish Records**

Search results are presented in a tabular format with an indication of pricing if you wish to view more detailed information.

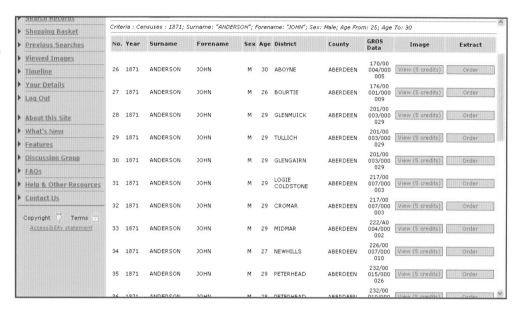

Criteria : Censuses : 1871; Surname: "ANDERSON"; Forename: "JOHN"; Sex: Male; Age From: 25; Age To: 30

No.	Year	Surname	Forename	Sex	Age	District	County	GRD5 Data	Image	Extract
26	1871	ANDERSON	JOHN	M	30	ABOYNE	ABERDEEN	170/00 004/000 005	View (5 credits)	Order
27	1871	ANDERSON	JOHN	M	26	BOURTIE	ABERDEEN	176/00 001/000 009	View (5 credits)	Order
28	1871	ANDERSON	JOHN	M	29	GLENMUICK	ABERDEEN	201/00 003/000 029	View (5 credits)	Order
29	1871	ANDERSON	JOHN	M	29	TULLICH	ABERDEEN	201/00 003/000 029	View (5 credits)	Order
30	1871	ANDERSON	JOHN	M	29	GLENGAIRN	ABERDEEN	201/00 003/000 029	View (5 credits)	Order
31	1871	ANDERSON	JOHN	M	29	LOGIE COLDSTONE	ABERDEEN	217/00 007/000 003	View (5 credits)	Order
32	1871	ANDERSON	JOHN	M	29	CROMAR	ABERDEEN	217/00 007/000 003	View (5 credits)	Order
33	1871	ANDERSON	JOHN	M	29	MIDMAR	ABERDEEN	222/A0 004/000 002	View (5 credits)	Order
34	1871	ANDERSON	JOHN	M	27	NEWHILLS	ABERDEEN	226/00 007/000 010	View (5 credits)	Order
35	1871	ANDERSON	JOHN	M	29	PETERHEAD	ABERDEEN	232/00 015/000 026	View (5 credits)	Order
36	1871	ANDERSON	JOHN	M	28	PETERHEAD	ABERDEEN	232/00 010/000	View (5 credits)	Order

The left navigation panel reads:
Search Records | Shopping Basket | Previous Searches | Viewed Images | Timeline | Your Details | Log Out | About this Site | What's New | Features | Discussion Group | FAQs | Help & Other Resources | Contact Us | Copyright Terms | Accessibility statement

any register entry (referred to as an 'extract'), you can do this online for a fixed fee of £10.

For Scottish family historians, there are also lots of useful features such as the glossary of old Scots words. For example, a bailiff is someone who protects fishing rights on a river rather than a person who collects payment for debt – the more modern usage of the word.

Use the glossary to make sure you don't misrepresent your ancestors.

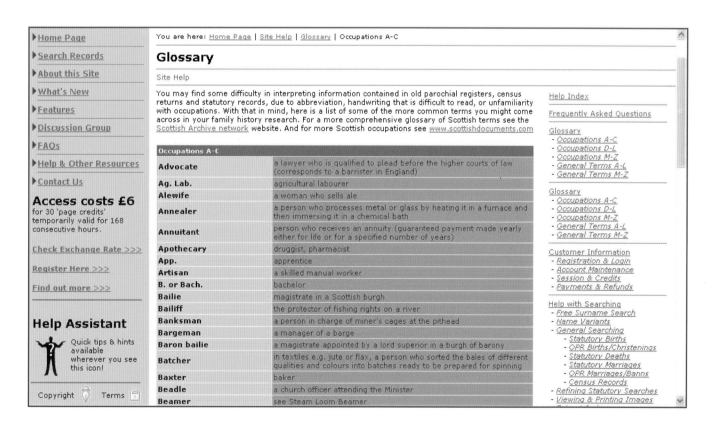

You are here: Home Page | Site Help | Glossary | Occupations A-C

Glossary

Site Help

You may find some difficulty in interpreting information contained in old parochial registers, census returns and statutory records, due to abbreviation, handwriting that is difficult to read, or unfamiliarity with occupations. With that in mind, here is a list of some of the more common terms you might come across in your family history research. For a more comprehensive glossary of Scottish terms see the Scottish Archive network website. And for more Scottish occupations see www.scottishdocuments.com

Occupations A-C	
Advocate	a lawyer who is qualified to plead before the higher courts of law (corresponds to a barrister in England)
Ag. Lab.	agricultural labourer
Alewife	a woman who sells ale
Annealer	a person who processes metal or glass by heating it in a furnace and then immersing it in a chemical bath
Annuitant	person who receives an annuity (guaranteed payment made yearly either for life or for a specified number of years)
Apothecary	druggist, pharmacist
App.	apprentice
Artisan	a skilled manual worker
B. or Bach.	bachelor
Bailie	magistrate in a Scottish burgh
Bailiff	the protector of fishing rights on a river
Banksman	a person in charge of miner's cages at the pithead
Bargeman	a manager of a barge
Baron bailie	a magistrate appointed by a lord superior in a burgh of barony
Batcher	in textiles e.g. jute or flax, a person who sorted the bales of different qualities and colours into batches ready to be prepared for spinning
Baxter	baker
Beadle	a church officer attending the Minister
Beamer	see Steam Loom Beamer

Left navigation panel:
Home Page | Search Records | About this Site | What's New | Features | Discussion Group | FAQs | Help & Other Resources | Contact Us

Access costs £6
for 30 'page credits' temporarily valid for 168 consecutive hours.

Check Exchange Rate >>>

Register Here >>>

Find out more >>>

Help Assistant
Quick tips & hints available wherever you see this icon!

Copyright Terms

Right navigation panel:
Help Index

Frequently Asked Questions

Glossary
- Occupations A-C
- Occupations D-L
- Occupations M-Z
- General Terms A-L
- General Terms M-Z

Glossary
- Occupations A-C
- Occupations D-L
- Occupations M-Z
- General Terms A-L
- General Terms M-Z

Customer Information
- Registration & Login
- Account Maintenance
- Session & Credits
- Payments & Refunds

Help with Searching
- Free Surname Search
- Name Variants
- General Searching
  - Statutory Births
  - OPR Births/Christenings
  - Statutory Deaths
  - Statutory Marriages
  - OPR Marriages/Banns
  - Census Records
- Refining Statutory Searches
- Viewing & Printing Images

PART

Other researchers

When you use the internet for genealogical research, it's impossible to ignore the contribution made by the Church of Jesus Christ of Latter-Day Saints (also known as the LDS Church or, more colloquially, the Mormons). The LDS Church maintains the largest collection of genealogical research in the world at its Family History Library in Salt Lake City, Utah, and its associated websites have records of an incredible 1.7 billion people – including 100 million people from England, Scotland, Wales and Ireland. Most importantly of all, the LDS Church shares its research with the entire world and you can add your research to its database. Before embarking on any difficult research project, it's a very good idea to check the LDS Church's records to see if one of its army of researchers has already done the hard work for you.

Why is genealogical research so important to LDS Church members? The Church believes that family love continues forever, even after death, and its members can perform temple 'ordinances' such as baptisms, promises to the Lord and family bindings on behalf of their deceased ancestors. Of course, before members can perform such ordinances they need to be able to identify their ancestors, which is where the genealogical research comes in. It's a win–win system: by sharing their records with the world, the LDS Church provides real benefits to researchers, who are then happy to return the favour and add their data to the LDS Church's database.

The role of the family is central to LDS Church beliefs.

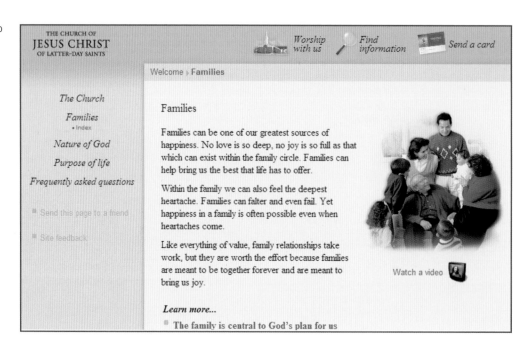

So what sort of information is available? Prepare to be amazed. For example, when we searched the RootsWeb site (**www.rootsweb.com**) for the name 'Charles Judd', we discovered Charles Henry 'Zhu Mingyang' Judd, a British Missionary who was born in 1842. According to RootsWeb, Charles was born in Loughborough and studied in Islington before becoming a missionary in China. Here's what the WorldConnect database says about him:

Charles Henry Judd, British missionary (male), was christened at All Saints, Loughborough, Leicestershire, England, on 26 July 1842, the son of Robert Judd and (Mrs.) Jane Judd.

Originally a bank clerk from Loughborough, he became a student at the Church Missionary Training College at Islington, London, preparing to join the CMS. However, he felt uncomfortable with infant baptism. He had attended meetings at Welbeck Street and knew the CMS missionary Frederick Gough. After the Lammermuir party had sailed for China, Judd became aware of the writings of Grattan Guinness, and at Gough's home in Bow, east London, met Thomas J. Barnardo. As a consequence, he became aware of J. Hudson Taylor's mission and left the CMS training institute. For about one year he lived with W. T. Berger at Saint Hill, near East Grinstead, Sussex, as a tutor in English. Having married in October 1867, Judd left for China with Mrs. Ann Bohannan, the Cardwells, and Edward Fishe. The party arrived in China on 3 March 1868.

In 1868 Judd was assigned to Yangzhou, Jiangsu; in 1869 to Zhenjiang, Jiangsu. He went to England on furlough in 1872 and returned in 1873. In 1874 he was at Wuchang, Hubei, with J. Hudson Taylor. In 1875, with two Chinese, he rented a house at Yuezhou [now Yueyang], Hunan, but was forced out by local Chinese. In 1877 he travelled with his brother-in-law J. F. Broumton through Hunan province to Guiyang, Guizhou, where the British adventurer William Mesny had facilitated the introduction of Christianity. While Broumton remained at Guiyang, Judd returned to Wuchang via Chongqing, Sichuan. In 1879 Judd established himself at Yantai [or Chefoo], Shandong, before the CIM school and sanatorium were established there.

Judd is recorded to have left China again between 1885 and May 1887. He left again in May 1894, with no date recorded of his return. Judd died in London, England, on 23 October 1919.

Charles Henry Judd married Elizabeth Jane Broumton in late 1867.

They had issue.

Death: 23 OCT 1919 in London, Middlesex, England, UK

Incredible, isn't it? And it doesn't stop there: where appropriate, each record links to that individual's ancestors and relatives. For example, Charles the missionary had a son; if we click his name, we can find out about him too:

George Judd F.R.G.S. (Fellow of the Royal Geographic Society), travelled extensively around the world at the turn of the century. G. Judd travelled through Indian, Kashmir, China, Korea, Japan, Africa, Egypt, Baghdad, Babylon, Jerusalem, Russia, Jamaica, Australia, & Tasmania.

It's fascinating stuff so don't be surprised if you end up spending days searching the RootsWeb database. But that's not all you can do: the RootsWeb site provides many ways to seek help or get advice from other researchers, such as by joining one or more of the mailing lists or by posting messages to the numerous message boards. You can also build a website: RootsWeb provides free webspace.

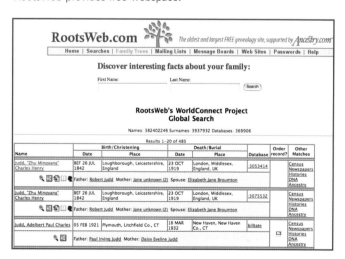

RootsWeb is a truly massive genealogy resource but while it's very big, it's also very easy to use. The site includes handy message boards and website building tools to make your life even easier.

INTERNET RESEARCH

Google Groups

Google Groups is a free online service that gives you access to the internet's most comprehensive archive of discussion groups. We're talking about Usenet: a global network of forums where people of like mind and common interest gather together to exchange messages. Usenet is less immediate than email, less personal than a chat room, and populated with geeks and self-publicists. But it's also a powerful research resource. With over a billion messages already in the archive, no matter what your question might be, you can bet that somebody somewhere has asked it before – and quite possibly had it answered.

What's in a name?

It all goes back to 1979 and a couple of American graduate students, Tom Truscott and Jim Ellis, who thought it might be jolly if two or more people could pool and share information with their computers. Thus they built a small network and used it to host a few electronic forums, each of which dealt with one specific topic (the vagaries of the Unix operating system, generally). Skip forward to the present day and what you find are well over 100,000 such forums. Known as newsgroups, most are open to anyone and together they cover every conceivable subject under the sun.

But with so many groups around, how do you find the right one(s) for you? Luckily, the potential anarchy of Usenet is somewhat tamed by a hierarchical structure. Newsgroup names are expressed as a series of words or phrases separated by dots. The first part locates a group's general field – **rec.** for recreation, **biz.** for business, **soc.** for social issues, and so on – and the rest is purely descriptive. Thus **soc.genealogy.britain** should be useful if you're researching your family tree, trout ticklers may prefer **rec.outdoors.fishing** and somebody somewhere presumably has a use for **alt.stupidity.spatch**. Note that 'alt.' prefix, incidentally. This stands for alternative and it's here that you'll find – or can choose to avoid – Usenet's seamier side.

However, beyond the helpful hierarchy, Google Groups makes life really simple by letting you search all or selected groups for key words. It's just like searching the web, in fact: enter your family name and perhaps a location or some other key word (like 'genealogy') and see what pops up. We can guarantee that you'll be amazed.

Alongside Usenet, Google also hosts its own discussion forums. Anybody can set up a Google Group and you can opt to make it public or private. Private groups work on the basis of membership, where only members can read and participate in discussions, whereas public groups are more akin to Usenet itself.

Using Google Groups

Getting to grips with Google Groups can be tricky at first because the interface is so unlike that of the web (although it has to be said that Google has made a tremendous job of making Usenet much more accessible than it once was). Here's a look at the basics.

Go to **http://groups-beta.google.com**. *Here you will find an option to join the service. However, this is not necessary if you want simply to search the archives; only when you want to post a message or join a group need you sign up. Enter a couple of key words in the search box and click Search Groups.*

The results page displays relevant posts (a post is a message in a group) with your key words conveniently highlighted. Click the blue headline to read a message in full and also to see any related messages. The green link below each message tells you which group it belongs to. Click a group link to go straight to that group. Play around here for an hour or two until you get the hang of it.

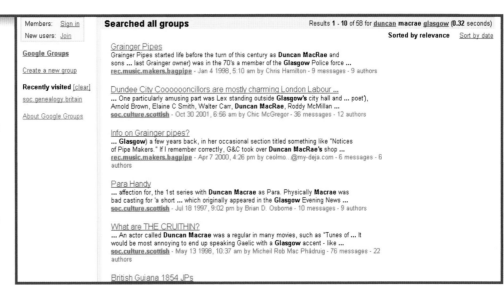

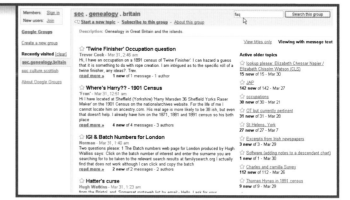

If you'd rather browse a group that's clearly related to your interests, go to the Google Groups homepage (or the My Groups page if you've already joined) and click a top-level category. You can use the search box within any specific category to keep refining the list of groups until you find what you're looking for. For instance, if you select 'Regions and Places' followed by 'People' followed by 'Genealogy', you'll find over 100 genealogy groups. One of them is **soc.genealogy.britain**. Click on the green link.

Here you will see the topics currently being discussed. Click any 'read more' link to open the message and see other related messages. It's also well worth looking for a group's FAQ (Frequently Asked Questions) file, which will tell you why the group was set up, what information you can hope to find, and what kind of questions are worth asking. Just enter 'faq' as a key word.

To post a message to any group, whether in Usenet or a public or private Google Group, you need to create a Google account. To do this, click the 'Join' button on the Google Group home page at **http://groups-beta.google.com**. Enter your email address and a password. A confirmation email will be sent to you straight away.

You can then join your chosen group by clicking the 'Subscribe to this group' link seen in the screenshot in Step 4. You will also now have a My Groups page which lists and keeps track of all the groups you have joined. Choose how you want to read messages posted to the group: by daily email or by accessing the group on the web as and when you choose.

Once you have joined a group, you can contribute to any discussion by clicking a topic title. This opens the entire discussion 'thread' (a thread is a list of related messages on a given subject displayed as a sequence in order of date). The list to the left side of the page details who has contributed to the discussion, and when. To reply to an existing message, click 'Reply' at the bottom of the message. A text box will open for you to type your message. Now click 'Post'. Your message will appear in seconds (unless the group is moderated, in which case it will have to be approved by the owner of the group).

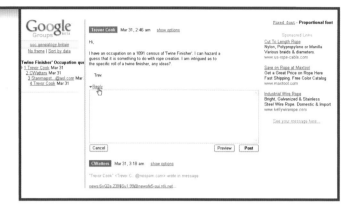

If you want to contact the author of a post directly, click the 'show options' button that appears next to the poster's name (as seen in the previous screenshot). A list of options will appear, one of which is 'Reply to Author'. Click this to open a message window. You can then add your comments and send the message to the author without it appearing in the group.

To the left of each topic heading is a star icon. If you click on this, it turns yellow and all new posts to that particular topic will automatically appear in your personal My Groups page. This is a handy way of keeping tabs on discussions that interest you.

You can also create a Google Group. This could be a really useful addition to your family history archive, as it allows relatives and friends to contribute to discussions about your family history and assist in your search for information. Make the group private if you want to limit access to people you know, and post a link to it on the home page of your family archive.

3

PART **3**

Fleshing out the bones

FLESHING OUT THE BONES

Photographs

One of the most rewarding additions to any collection of dates is a simple photograph. It's all very well knowing that Great Auntie Jeannie was a seamstress in Sunderland in 1912 but isn't it just as fascinating knowing what she looked like? You can be sure of one thing: if you want to get children involved in building your family archive – and we strongly suggest that you should – then you'll have to give them more to get their teeth into than dates alone.

Snap happy

Within the context of a family, old photographs are priceless. One of the things you can do with your archive is preserve these photos for future generations. Don't underestimate the importance of this: photographs decay and fade with age; they are highly vulnerable to accidental damage; and they don't take kindly to excessive handling.

It's also important to put names to faces in photographs, and the best time to do this is now – while you still can. Ask older relatives for this information and store it now before it is lost forever.

By digitally preserving your family photos, you are also safeguarding your heritage against any future catastrophe, such as house fire, flood, burglary, loss during a house move, or photographs getting accidentally thrown out with the rubbish

Once scanned, old family photographs can be enjoyed by the whole family rather than lying forgotten in some old shoe box. The original photos can then be carefully archived in a dry, dark, secure storage place, protected from any further deterioration.

Don't just think about photos of people for your archive. You can include photos of houses where family lived, favourite holiday destinations, a family car or dog, and any old heirlooms and mementos.

As a courtesy, you should check with family members still

There's nothing like an old family photo to stir the memory of relatives.

living before you publish their photos into an online archive. Not everybody appreciates the limelight. Also be careful when sourcing third-party images, as these are almost always subject to copyright restrictions. Don't just download pictures from somebody else's website and stick them in your family tree.

First steps

Gather together as many family portraits as you can find, ideally at least one for each member of your family tree. Show photographs to older relatives to see if they can remember any of the faces and names. Ask relatives for any family photos they may have. It is amazing how many families have at least one shoebox full of old black and white photos, and gratifying to see how much people enjoy reliving their memories.

Old photographs need to be handled and stored carefully. The less they are handled, the better, so treat them with respect.

To preserve a photograph, you should scan it. This involves nothing more than taking a photograph of it using a cheap and easy-to-use device called a scanner. The end result is a digital file on your computer. This is a faithful representation of the original, and it can be easily backed up, copied, edited, enhanced, enlarged or reduced, emailed, published online and otherwise manipulated to your heart's content. With a little practice, you can restore damaged sections of a photograph; and with a little experimentation, you can apply all manner of special effects. Once scanned, the original photo need never be handled again.

A website with lots of useful advice about how to scan and digitally preserve your family photos can be found here: **www.city-gallery.com/digital/scan-steps.php**. You'll find technical help with how to scan and get the best digital image from an old photograph, plus advice on cataloguing your photos and presenting them on your website. The site also covers the scanning of slides.

With a transparency adapter, you can scan slides as well as prints.

Schools

Once the family portraits are in place, you can add all kinds of other photographs to the tree. How about old school photographs, for example? Try a web search for a school or for the local historical society for that area. You may find a website with old class photographs.

Buildings and places

If you are trying to identify a particular place within a known region, try sending a scan of your photo to the relevant local history society. To get you started, go to **www.genuki.org.uk/big** and check out the links for each county and region of the UK.

It is also worth taking a look at this commercial site: **www.pastpix.com**. You'll find an online catalogue of over 20,000 historical photographs, mainly from the British Isles. There is no charge to look through the indexed catalogue and you may find some clues there to help you with dating your photographs. More on dating photos coming up.

The PastPix catalogue is very comprehensive and allows you to search by decade within each category.

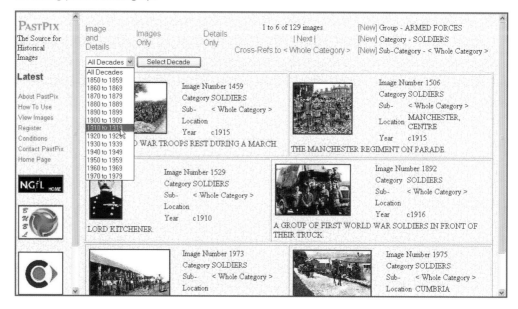

Why not show the passage of time by having contrasting photos of past and present family homes in your archive? You can either use existing photos or take new ones if this is possible.

For photos of towns, streets or areas within Britain, try local libraries. They usually hold collections of photographic material.

Then and now: the changing face of a street over the decades.

On Glasgow's Mitchell Library website, each photo is captioned and can be clicked for an enlarged version with further information.

This material is increasingly being made available online, and local history societies often hold a wealth of photographic material that can be viewed and scanned.

We have already mentioned **www.genuki.org.uk/big** as a good source of links to societies working at the county level of the UK. City collections are also beginning to appear online. A huge collection of photographs of London can be found at **www.photolondon.org.uk**. For Glasgow, go to **www.mitchelllibrary.org/vm**.

Or, of course, simply search Google or Google Images (**http://images.google.com**) for the name of your home town. Throw in a couple of key words like 'historical' and 'photos' for best results.

We can also recommend, the Francis Frith collection: **www.francisfrith.com**. This is a commercial site with old photographs of over 7,000 UK towns and villages plus historical maps and aerial photographs. If you find an image you would like to share with visitors to your online family tree, you can set up a direct link from your website to the Francis Frith site.

Graves

You could take photographs of family gravestones for your archive. So many gravestones are either worn away or have been vandalized, and so many cemeteries are either neglected or being sold, that this may be the only way to preserve such important historical information.

Not a cheery photo, perhaps, but possibly deserving of a place in your archive.

Weddings and special occasions

Why not take or find photos of churches where family members were married and have a family wedding section on your archive website, placing wedding photos alongside pictures of the churches? Sometimes original wedding dresses can still be found stuffed away in the back of wardrobes. Get them out, shake them down and take a photo. You might also digitally preserve a family christening gown before it finally falls apart and gets turned into a duster. Try comparing two wedding photos – one old and one contemporary – to see the difference in clothing styles.

What about your dad's first baby shoe or your grandfather's old school cap? There are probably many trinkets and souvenirs that family members have kept and treasured over the years. If they can be found, they can be photographed.

Updating photographs

Don't forget to update the photos of children on the family tree as they grow. The traditional annual school photo would be a good one to use. Ask relatives to send you one each year. Also include photos of each new wedding and new arrival in the family. Once your family archive website is up and running, it will be easy to add new photos.

PART  # Dating old photographs

If you are lucky, you'll find that relatives will have written dates, names and locations on the back of their photos. This tradition appears to have all-but died out these days, which is a great shame for future historians. However, if you find a photo that you can't immediately place, it's time to turn detective.

Up close and personal

First, scan the original photo. You can then email a copy to any relative who might be able to help, or of course print copies and post them.

You can also try to date the photo yourself. First, use a magnifying glass and search the photograph for any detail that could help: the style of clothing, accessories, shoes, hairstyles, props used in the photograph, and so forth. Are there any shop signs or backdrops, any forms of transport, any buildings or types of architecture that could provide a clue?

The clue is in the detail and there are a number of online sites that can give advice and point you in the right direction.

A great starting point is the BBC family history site, which we've already mentioned. You'll find it here: **www.bbc.co.uk/history/community/family.** This site has an archive of hundreds of old photographs which you can compare with your own.

For instance, take a look at this page for help with dating Victorian studio portraits: **www.bbc.co.uk/history/your_history/family/victorian_photo1.shtml.**

For further general help with dating an old photograph, try **www.ajmorris.com/roots/photo**. Here you will find much sound advice and guidance on what to look for.

Learn how to examine your old photographs for dating clues.

Victorian studio photographs
By Susannah Davis

Discovering old photographs whilst researching your family can be of tremendous help. Examining fashions, photographic processes, studio details and themes of the photographs can offer some fascinating clues.

The early processes

 Before 1860, the photographic processes were daguerreotype (1840 to 1850) followed by the collodion process (1850 to 1860). The daguerreotype was exposed directly on to a silver-coated copper plate and no negative was involved. When turned in the light, daguerreotypes seem to turn negative in appearance and are generally no more than a few inches across. The collodion print began as a glass negative, but by 1852, its inventor came up with a method that produced "positives - by bleaching the negative, backing it with black paper, cloth or black varnish and placing it in a frame. Collodion prints are called ambrotypes in the USA. Daguerreotypes were very expensive; if you have a daguerreotype of one of your relatives, you can at least be sure they were very well to do! Collodion prints were much cheaper, but due to their fragility and their brief reigns of popularity, both formats are rarer than later paper prints, and are quite easy to date.

The later processes

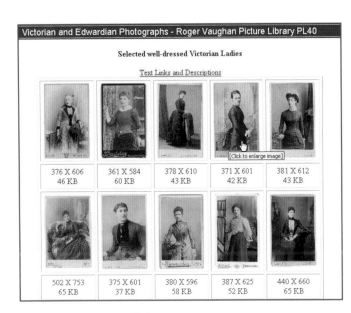

Browsing online photo galleries can help you identify and date your photographs.

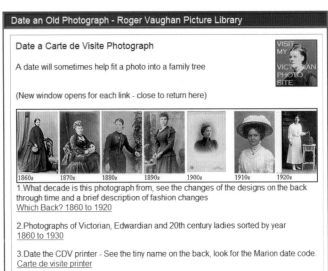

If he has the time, Roger Vaughan will have a go at dating a mystery Victorian photo for a small charge.

Many old photographs carry the photographer's imprint, and sometimes there may even be a date if you look very closely. If you have the name of a photographer and his studio, you might be able to find out the years during which he was working there. This site holds lists of Victorian and Edwardian photographers together with a dating calculator to help you pinpoint the decade in which a postcard was taken: **www.users.waitrose.com/~rodliffe/dating.html**.

For an alphabetical list of British photographers working between 1855 and 1901 and for help tracking down their studios, see: **http://mywebpage.netscape.com/hibchris/instant/aboutme.html**.

Clothing can often be an excellent indicator of date, as women's fashion changed quite regularly and even the poorest women would attempt to keep up with the trends for a photograph, even if it was simply by way of an accessory or a hairstyle. For hundreds of online sample fashion photographs covering the period from 1860 to 1930, see: **www.cartes.freeuk.com/time/date.htm**.

If your detective work draws a blank, go to **www.rogerco.freeserve.co.uk**. You can submit a scan of a photograph and get it dated by an expert for a cost of £4 (email first to request this service). You can also purchase vintage photographs here to attach to your website.

Some dating examples

Here are three examples to illustrate just how to go about dating a photograph. The first step is always to find some detail to use as the starting point. Often, it's clothing that gives the game away.

1. Victorian couple In this photo it was the sleeve on the woman's jacket that held the clue. After consulting **www.ajmorris.com/roots/photo** and **www.cartes.freeuk.com/time/date.htm**, we learned that the jacket has a very particular stylistic feature, namely the 'mutton leg' sleeve. This first appeared around 1891, peaked in 1896 and was gone by 1900. This makes it highly probable that the photograph was taken in the 1890s, as ladies would always have worn their most fashionable clothes for an important photograph.

Having then consulted Fashion-era (**www.fashion-era.com**), we also discovered that upper-class ladies began wearing suits made of tweed or wool in the late 1880s and that the style then filtered down through the classes. By the turn of the century, a tailored suit was an accepted and common-place garment for women from all walks of life. To avoid it appearing too masculine, a lacy blouse would sometimes be worn – as indeed can be seen here.

2. Edwardian lady The blouse seemed to hold the clue here. After some searching on **www.fashion-era.com**, we found a page dedicated to the detailing used on blouses during the Edwardian period. This lady's blouse perfectly matched the description given there and we could conclude that this photo was taken around 1910.

Fashion Era is an American site owned and run by Pauline Weston Thomas and Guy Thomas. You can seek Pauline's help with any fashion queries in return for an online donation made through PayPal (**www.paypal.com**).

The 'mutton leg' sleeve is a giveaway in this photo.

Our forgotten relative apparently posed for this photo c.1910.

Find a match to find a date.

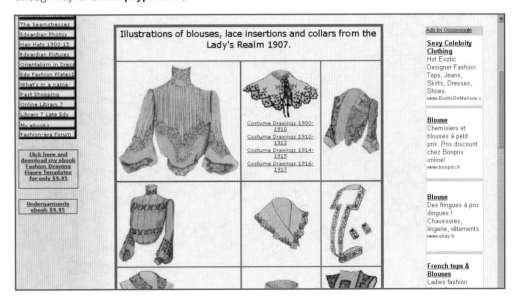

It's a handsome beast but who owned it and when was this photograph taken?

The scanned photo is pixilated and grainy when thus enlarged but the distinctive badge is unmistakably that of a Wolseley.

3. Old Car This was a real puzzler. We asked around and learned from one relative that the car *might* have belonged to a Parish Minister in Scotland. But this was a long shot and she could provide no further information.

The photograph was so small that it was impossible to identify the make of the vehicle (if you know absolutely nothing about cars, that is). But by scanning the photo at the highest resolution and them zooming in, we could provide sufficient details for a friend to confidently identify the badge as that of the Wolseley marque.

Thus armed, we paid a visit to **www.oldclassiccar.co.uk**, a website with photographs of hundreds of cars dating from the 1930s to the 1970s plus loads of other information abut the Golden Age of motoring. It's run and maintained by an enthusiast who welcomes additions to his already vast collection.

This site had three Wolseleys listed in the 1930s.

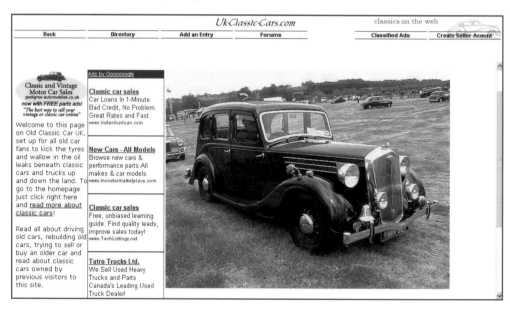

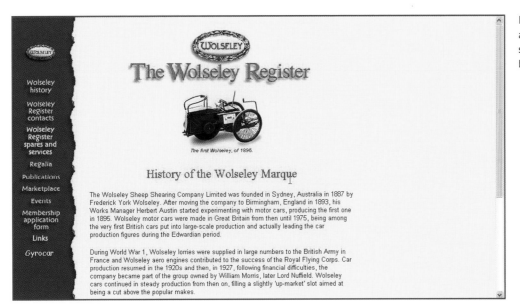

It's amazing how often you'll find a website dedicated to a single subject, run by enthusiasts and brimming with useful information.

The first Wolseley we found looked like a perfect match for our mystery photograph. Interestingly enough, it appears that the model in question was used for police cars at that time. This clearly required further investigation!

We then searched on Google (**www.google.com**) for more information about Wolseleys and came across a website dedicated to the marque: **www.wolseley.dircon.co.uk/contents.html**. This confirmed that Wolseley did indeed make police cars. We also discovered that the distinctive Wolseley radiator badge visible on the front of our car did not come into production until 1932, so that was our first solid clue.

To try to pin down the year, we turned our attention to the registration number. A Google search eventually led to both **http://fleetdata.co.uk/ukregistrations.html** and **http://en.wikipedia.org/wiki/British_car_number_plates.** Here we found detailed explanations of the car registration system, along with tables recording all the single, double and three letter combinations issued by the various authorities in the UK.

Here's a summary of the relevant section from the Wikipedia article (this article in its original form is licensed under the GNU Free Documentation License, see **www.gnu.org/copyleft/fdl.html**):

Before 1932
The first series of number plates were issued in 1903 and ran until 1932, using the series A1–YY9999. The letter or pair of letters indicated the local area where the vehicle was registered, for example, A – London, B – Lancashire, C – West Riding of Yorkshire, etc. In England and Wales the letter codes were initially allocated in order of population size (by the 1901 census), whilst Scotland and Ireland had special sequences incorporating the letters 'S' and 'I' respectively, which were allocated alphabetically: IA = Antrim, IB = Armagh, etc. When a licensing authority reached 9999, it was allocated another two letter mark, but there was no pattern to these subsequent allocations.

1932 to 1963
By 1932, the available numbers within this scheme were running out, and an extended scheme was introduced. This scheme consisted of three letters and three numbers, taken from the series AAA1 to YYY999. Note that certain letters – I, Q and Z – were never used, as they were considered too easy to mistake for other letters or numbers, or were reserved for special use, such as the use of I and Z for Irish registrations. (After independence, the Irish Republic continued to use this scheme until 1986.)

The three letter scheme preserved the area letter codes as the second pair of letters in the set of three, and the single letter area codes were deleted (since prefixing a single letter code would create a duplicate of a two-letter code). In some areas, the available numbers with this scheme started to run out in the 1950s, and in those areas, a reversed sequence was introduced, i.e. 1AAA-999YYY. The ever-increasing popularity of the car can be gauged by noting that these sequences ran out within ten years, and by the beginning of the 1960s, a further change was made in very popular areas, introducing 4-number sequences with the one and two letter area codes, but in the reverse direction to the early scheme – i.e. 1A-9999YY.

We now know where the car was first registered: the first letter tells us that it was registered in Scotland and the second letter tells us (after some more searching) that it was registered in the district of Morayshire. This confirms the suspected Scottish connection.

We now have a puzzle, though, as the two letter prefix would suggest that the car was pre-1932 but we already know that it has to be later than that because of the radiator badge. Confirmation of the model might assist with the dating process.

Some more searching uncovers a number of Wolseley sites set up by enthusiasts, some with galleries of photographs. A little browsing confirms that our car appears to date from the late 1930s.

If you get really stuck, you can try sending your photo to one of the sites maintained by car enthusiasts. We emailed a scan of our car photograph to **www.oldclassiccar.co.uk**. The site editor responded within the hour and confirmed that it was indeed a Wolseley (very reassuring) but definitely not a police car because police cars were always black with a bell on the front bumper and ours was two-tone and bell-less. He dated it as probably late 1930s. Just to be sure, we then emailed the photo to the Surrey Vintage Vehicle Society: **www.svvs.org**. On the Help Page, members attempt to identify cars from photos sent in by the public. This service is provided on an amateur basis free of charge. Our enquiry drew this response:

> *As far as your photo is concerned, quick identification is that the car is Wolseley. From the lower slung headlights and smaller dip in the bumper it is probably a Series II. It looks beefy so it is probably a 18/80 and from the mudguards flowing into the running boards, it has a Salon de Ville body. These were built between 1936 and 1938. The car was registered in Morayshire.*

So…in the space of 48 hours and without even leaving our desk, we have identified the make and model, confirmed the suspected Scottish connection, and verified that the car dates from the late 1930s (that oddity about the registration number notwithstanding – perhaps Morayshire stuck with the old numbering system into the 1940s).

This licence plate reads SO 6546.
Surely a clue there?

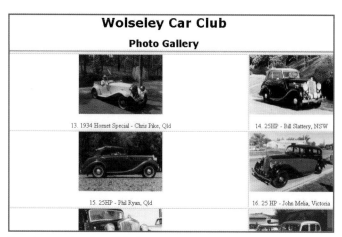

Search around and you'll find
plenty of photos of old cars.

Get help dating cars from the
Surrey Vintage Vehicle Society.

PART 3 Adding colour

Let's continue this theme of expanding the family tree beyond the inclusion of mere dates and data. Anything you gather now can play a part in your family archive later when you come to build your website and publish it on the internet.

Paper trail

As you trace your family tree you will gradually accumulate a number of official documents. Birth, marriage and death certificates are the main ones. These can all be scanned and included in your online family tree.

You will find that these certificates contain a lot of very interesting information. For instance, a birth certificate should tell you the full names of the parents, the occupation of the father

and the address where the mother was living at the time of the birth. A marriage certificate will have the names and occupations of the fathers of both the bride and the groom. All of this helps to piece together your family history and will be of interest to other family members when they look at the online family tree.

Talk to older relatives about your project and you'll likely be given letters, newspaper cuttings, tickets, diaries, postcards, old school books and reports, favourite family recipes, Christmas and birthday cards, and all manner of other items which can be photographed or scanned and added to your archive. Think in terms of an online scrapbook (see p150).

Scanning old documents also acts to preserve them. Paper documents decay, inks fade, and handwriting gradually becomes impossible to decipher. By scanning them now, you can help ensure that future generations will be able to enjoy these valuable heirlooms.

This is a copy of an original birth certificate from 1885.

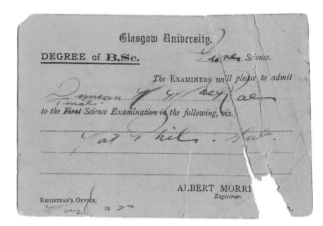

If it can be scanned and has meaning to somebody, stick it in the archive with a brief explanation.

Those old novelty snapshots deserve a place in your archive.

First shoes, lasting memories.

Grandad's old watch, awarded for 40 years of service (perhaps) and now immortalised online.

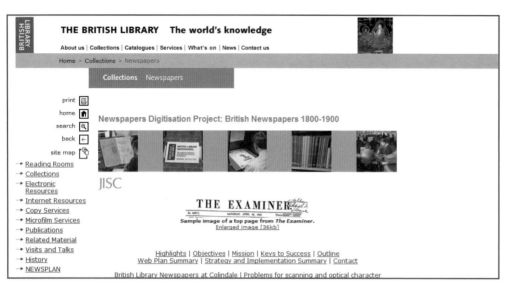

print
home
search
back
site map

→ Reading Rooms
→ Collections
→ Electronic Resources
→ Internet Resources
→ Copy Services
→ Microfilm Services
→ Publications
→ Related Material
→ Visits and Talks
→ History
→ NEWSPLAN

Newspapers Digitisation Project: British Newspapers 1800-1900

JISC

THE EXAMINER

Sample image of a top page from *The Examiner*.
Enlarged image [36kb]

Highlights | Objectives | Mission | Keys to Success | Outline
Web Plan Summary | Strategy and Implementation Summary | Contact
British Library Newspapers at Colindale | Problems for scanning and optical character

The British Library's Digitisation Project will eventually see a century's worth of newspapers scanned for the web.

If you have old newspaper clippings lurking in a drawer, promote them to your archive.

Newspapers

The British Library holds the largest collection of old newspapers in Britain. Details can be found on its website at **www.bl.uk/collections/newspapers.html**. It is not possible to do online searches of newspapers, though; you have to show up in person. However, the Library is in the process of digitising up to two million pages of British national, regional and local newspapers from between 1800 and 1900. Access to these will eventually be offered on the internet, albeit limited to students.

The American site **www.newspaperarchive.com** contains scans of over 21 million newspaper pages, with a few going as far back as 1753. There are only 12 British newspapers listed, however, of which five are Edinburgh titles. The other countries covered are Canada, Ireland, Denmark and Jamaica. The big downside to this site is the cost. You have to pay a monthly fee of just under $18 to access any information, and copies of newspaper pages cost around $30 each (plus postage). Pages are printed onto cotton for framing as a keepsake or gift, but this isn't ideal when you want to include a page in your website!

A free alternative site is operated by the American Library of Congress: **www.loc.gov/rr/news/oltitles.html**. Run by volunteers, it provides a very comprehensive list of newspapers throughout the world with online archives. Of the USA newspapers listed, several have online archives going back over 100 years: *Washington Post* from 1877; *New York Times* from 1851; *Cleveland Press* from 1878; and *New York Tribune* from 1875. In the UK section, which includes Ireland, there are 21 newspapers, but the oldest archive there is *The Times* and *Sunday Times*, which goes back only to 1985.

Only one UK paper has a searchable archive online going back more than 20 years, and that is the *Scotsman*. Every edition of the newspaper from 1817–1910 has been scanned and can be viewed and online, with plans to eventually bring it right up to the present day.

To buy an archived newspaper, go to **www.remember-when.co.uk**. This site has papers spanning over 350 years from 1642 to the present day. Prices start at £24.95.

For local newspapers go to **www.genuki.org.uk/big/Newspapers.html**. There you will find links to national and local newspapers online.

Folk

Messing About on the River,
Tron Theatre, Glasgow
Rob Adams

MUSIC before Josh McRae was, said Danny Kyle, muck. Well, not muck exactly, but another word that aptly sums up songs such as *I'm A Pink Toothbrush, You're A Blue Toothbrush*. McRae took Kyle and many others away from that and into a world populated by blues singers, dust bowls, and cowboys. Especially cowboys.

Onstage alongside Kyle were half a dozen others who knew McRae well. A show of hands in the audience suggested that they were mostly among friends. It was that sort of night — intimate, occasionally ramshackle, and a bloke in the audience who'd obviously heard of the Glaswegians' reputation for heckling. Drawing on the cowboy connection, Kyle shot him down.

When he could get his tongue in sideways Kyle gave us a verbal picture of the conundrum that was Josh McRae. Two songs, sung back to back by McRae's daughter Kirsty, illustrated the range of the songs he sang. A daft wee ditty about the wee ferry boat, HMS Back'n'Forward, was followed by a letter home from a prisoner on death row set to music by Pete Seeger.

McRae didn't write many songs. But he could choose them — for himself and other people. And not only did he introduce aspiring singers to Americana, he showed them what their own tradition had to offer, from the *Recruiting Sergeant* (an odd choice for a dyed-in-the-wool pacifist) to the travelling people songs of Jeannie Robertson.

"Wish he'd taken his own advice," said Kyle, introducing a song about the dangers of whisky. A sobering moment, but it was the only one in a show that paid entertaining and affectionate tribute to a genuine character.

JOSH McRAE
An appreciation

My reaction to the recent death of Josh McRae, the singer, strong though it was, must be shared by a great many people throughout Scotland and beyond.

I spent my student years at the Glasgow School of Art with Josh, and he was the first person I ever heard actually play the guitar. At that time, he played blues very much in the style of the late Josh White, thus earning the name which stayed with him for the rest of his life. In my first year as a student, two people at the Art School played guitar. I was the other. When I graduated four years later, there were at least 20.

Even now, people still know the songs that Josh made famous, and when Yuri Gagarin made the first space flight, Roddy McMillan's song, sung by Josh, went round a delighted world, and became a colossal hit in Russia.

Josh McRae's contribution in the very earliest days of the folk music revival in this country cannot be over-estimated. He had plans for a return to performing, and it is tragic that they never came to fruition, for there is no doubt that he still had a great deal to offer. Josh McRae had, in full measure, those qualities which I value most highly, and so readily in my folk friends, warmth and h...

Jimmie M...

MACRAE — Peacefully, at home, 7 Hillcrest Avenue, Carsmyle on 20th June 1975, DUNCAN N M MACRAE, retired head master (formerly of Ashcroft Drive, Glasgow, G44) dear husband of the late Ishobel, dear father of Roderick Iain, and Sheila, and dear friend of Helen.—Funeral service at Linn Crematorium Lainshaw Drive, Glasgow, G45, on Monday 23rd inst. at 12 noon; no flowers or letters please.

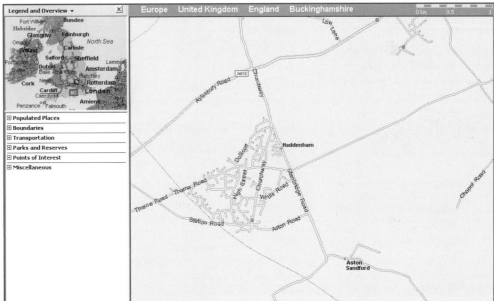

The village of Haddenham as it looked then, as it looks now, and as it looks from above.

The image above has been derived from 2m resolution aerial photography supplied by **Getmapping plc**.

Maps

Addresses for your ancestors can be found on birth, marriage and death certificates, and on the 1901 online census. Armed with this information, you could plot locations on a map to gain an idea of their movements.

Modern maps can be viewed and searched online with the likes of Multimap (**www.multimap.com**) and Google Maps (**http://maps.google.co.uk**). You could use these to plot where people were born, or take one ancestor and plot all the stages of his or her life on one map, from birth through marriage to death. We'll do just that on p75.

A family member who fought in a war overseas would make an interesting subject, as would any family member who emigrated. You may find that you need a map of the world in order to illustrate just how far your family has grown from its original roots.

Haddenham at the beginning of
the 19th century.

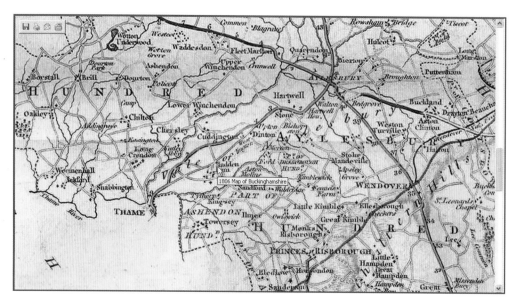

To search historical maps, go to **www.old-maps.co.uk**. This is
Britain's most extensive digital map archive, and you can search
for a place or a specific address. Once you have found a location,
you can view an historical map, a modern map or in many cases
an aerial photograph. It's fascinating to see just how landscapes
change.

You may download a maximum of 10 images from the site for
use on personal web pages providing you credit the source. You
can also purchase decorative copies of historical maps.

For county maps, **www.genuki.org.uk/big** is an excellent
source. This takes you straight to the UK and Ireland section
where you can select a country and a county and then check
which maps are available. A search for Haddenham provided a
choice of several maps dating from 1806.

You can also try local government and council websites and
local historical societies. Haddenham, our current target, is in
Buckinghamshire, and there is a Buckinghamshire Genealogical
Society to be found at **www.bucksgs.org.uk**. On checking this
site, we found more maps of the area plus a big selection of
modern photographs showing how the various villages and towns
look today. There are 16 photographs of buildings in the village
of Haddenham alone.

Seek out present-day photographs
of places where your ancestors
lived to bring your family history
to life.

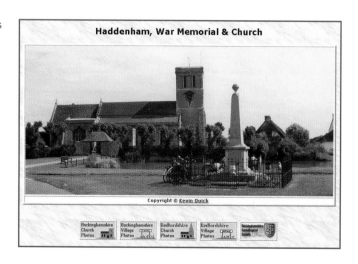

Occupations

Official certificates can provide you with a lot of information about the occupations of your ancestors. You may recognise an occupation – baker or shoemaker, for example – but some trades may be unfamiliar to you.

There are several online sites that can provide definitions of these obscure professions. Try **www.gendocs.demon.co.uk/trades.html**, for starters. Many of these old words are still used in modern day English, albeit with slightly different meanings:

a henter – a thief
a tippler – a person who worked in an alehouse
a bummer – an army deserter
a busker – a hairdresser
a nob thatcher – a wig maker
a nimgimmer – a doctor
a piker – a tramp or vagrant
a snobscat – a shoe repairer
a streaker – person who prepared bodies for burial
a wanter – a mole catcher
a clod hopper – a ploughman
a turnkey – a prisonwarder
a tweenie – a junior maid who assisted the cooks.

For very old and now obsolete occupations going back to medieval times, try **www.olivetreegenealogy.com/misc/occupations.shtml**.

Here you will discover that a spittleman was a hospital attendant and a fletcher was an arrow maker.

Once you have an occupation, you can search the web for more information about what the work was like, conditions, salaries, and what that person's status would have been within the community. For instance, the National Archives website, **www.nationalarchives.gov.uk/pathways/exhibitions.htm,** has two illustrated exhibitions – *First World War* and *1901: Living at the Time of the Census* – that give a real insight to life during those particular times.

Many professions and trades had their own associations, colleges or societies, some of which still exist today. Craft guilds – voluntary associations for particular craftsmen – were formed as far back as the Middle Ages. The most famous guilds were the London ones, called livery companies. The Worshipful Company of Fletchers (arrow makers) is a good example and you can read all about their history on their website **www.fletchers.org.uk/frames/navframe.html**.

For a complete list of all the livery companies and links to individual sites, go to **www.cityoflondon.gov.uk/Corporation/ leisure_heritage/livery/linklist.htm**.

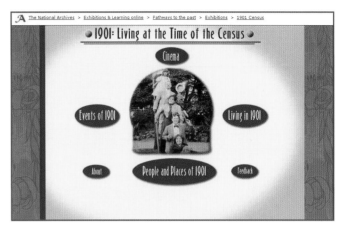

The combination of words, pictures and documents really brings to life how people were living at the time of the 1901 census.

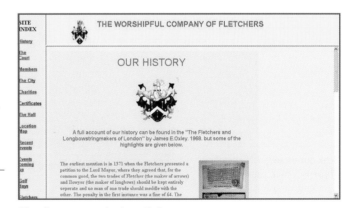

Most livery companies have their own website where you can read their history and see their coats of arms.

Military memories

It is likely that at some point one or more of your ancestors will have fought in a war. Are there any medals or other memorabilia that you could photograph? Would grandad be happy to talk about his experiences and share his memories?

Searching online

To identify Victorian and earlier military uniforms, try **www.thinred.co.uk**. This is an online shop that accurately replicates uniforms for purchase, but which also has an online Uniform Museum containing many pictures of uniforms from the Crimea to the Boer Wars.

You can also find numerous official and unofficial sites dedicated to specific regiments, many of which hold useful information and photographic material.

The only searchable online list of war personnel currently available is at **www.cwgc.org**, run by the Commonwealth War Graves Commission. This site has a database of 1.7 million service men and women from the Commonwealth who died in the two world wars, plus a database of over 67,000 civilians who died in World War Two.

Information about particular forces can be found through the Ministry of Defence site at **www.mod.uk**. Click on the army, navy or air force icon at the bottom of the page to take you to the relevant division, and then try to track down the specific regiment or ship you are interested in. You will not find any information about individuals here but it will provide further insight into your relative's life.

A family member in uniform.

You can search for the name and details of any individual who died during the two world wars.

World War I

For a wonderful resource of all things military, especially World War One, go here: **www.btinternet.com/~prosearch**. This site is owned and run by Tom Tulloch-Marshall, and he is able to undertake military genealogical research on your behalf (for a fee). The site is extremely informative and Tom gives a full run down of the type of information he does – and does not – need from you in order to conduct a search for a particular individual.

Another good site for background and context is www.worldwar1.com. This titles itself 'an internet History of the Great War' and is packed with information, photographs, maps, testimonials and many other fascinating sections.

World War II

For World War Two, you cannot do better than **www.bbc.co.uk/dna/ww2/Research**. This is an excellent site that provides a wealth of information about World War Two plus loads of advice abut how to research your family's involvement.

To look up which awards, medals and commendations a family member might have received during the world wars, try **www.gazettes-online.co.uk**. The *London*, *Edinburgh* and *Belfast Gazettes* are the official newspapers of record for the armed forces in the United Kingdom. Here you can access searchable online archives of the complete gazettes, containing medal awards, army and navy commissions, promotions and much more. If you are researching a family member who served during the wars or who was awarded a medal, this is a useful resource. However, you do need to have accurate starting information – dates, full names, regiments etc.– in order to get meaningful results.

Identifying medals

There are several good sites that can help you identify medals. This is useful if you have a photograph of an ancestor (or suspected ancestor) in uniform but you don't have a name or any other details; or even if some unidentified medals have been left as a family heirloom. Medals and other military insignia can help pin somebody down to a particular time and place in history, possibly even to a specific regiment.

To get started, try **www.militarybadges.org.uk**. This a free site with hundreds of photographs of British military badges and medals. You'll also find over 4,500 photographs of unidentified military personnel grouped in various collections.

Also check out **www.asacaustralia.com/mint3.htm,** an Australian site but one with a good selection of British medals.

Another Australian site – **http://ahoy.tk-jk.net/macslog/WorldWar2CampaignStarsand.html** – is actually a weblog run by a veteran, and it gives an excellent explanation of all the different medals awarded.

But the best site by far that we came across is **www.hallofmedals.co.uk**. This is run by a British medal enthusiast who has placed his entire collection online, all catalogued by conflict and by country, and photographed in colour with full explanations.

Finally, **www.militarystore.com.au** is a commercial site for purchasing military memorabilia, but you can browse through the different sections full of colour photographs of various medals, each with histories about why, where and when a medal was awarded.

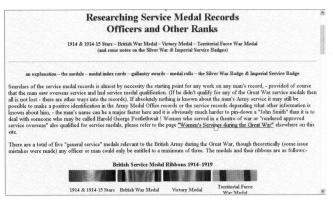

Lots of information here about great-grandad's war medals.

The BBC helps you research your family's involvement in the last world war.

With a little rooting around online, you should be able to identify medals and military insignia.

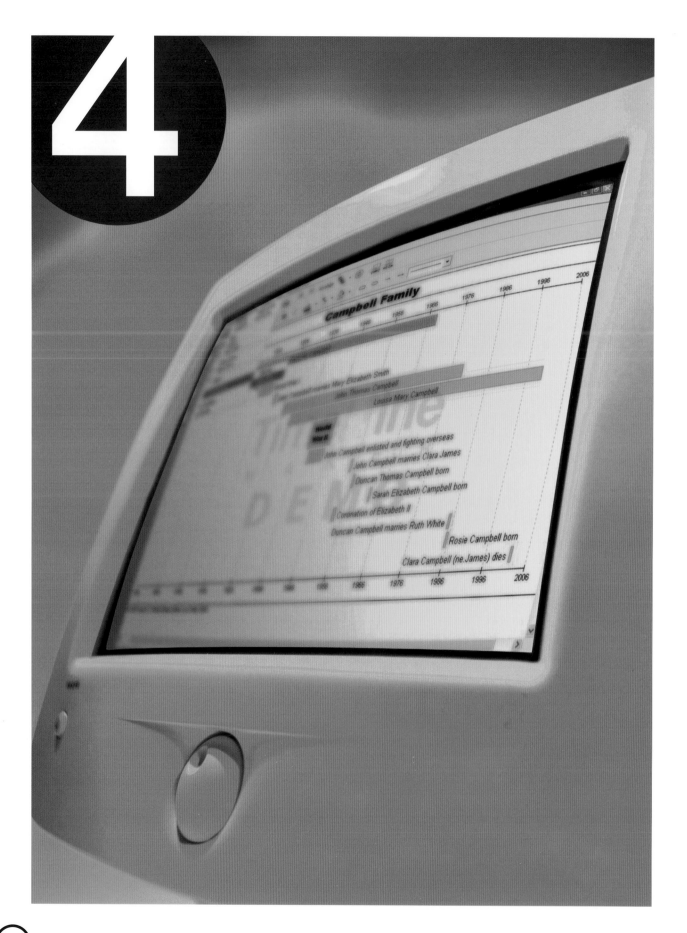

PART **4** INTERNET GENEALOGY MANUAL
Multimedia projects

Make a timeline

A timeline is a great way to chart the history of your family and to place it in context of wider events. Your timeline should show significant family events – when people were born, married and died, moved from one town to another, and so forth – and should also include the current events for that time at local, national or even world level. For instance, the life of a female ancestor might coincide with the Suffragette Movement, and occupations will always be interesting in the light of the industrial revolution.

One step at a time

A timeline can run either horizontally or vertically and can be divided into sections to make it more manageable. You might want to work on the basis of decades, or longer periods of history such as the Victorian or Edwardian eras. The idea is to plot your family's significant dates in chronological order along this line. You can then add other significant dates to bring the period more closely into focus: when an important medicine or invention was first introduced, the dates of battles or wars, the sinking of the *Titanic*, changes in Royalty, local events relevant to the part of the country from where your ancestors came, and just about anything else that takes your fancy. It's all a question of context and bringing your family history to life. Record anything that you feel would have had an impact on the lives of your ancestors. You might prefer to compile a separate timeline for each generation.

For a superb illustration of how informative timelines can be, and how to set them up on the web to make them easy to read, go to the Harry Potter Lexicon at **www.hp-lexicon.org/timeline.html**. This is a site dedicated to Harry Potter and provides both a master timeline for the whole Harry Potter saga and a number of smaller, more specialised timelines on topics such as the 'Chronology of the Sports Broom' and 'History of Quidditch'.

A crash course in wizard history courtesy of the Harry Potter Lexicon.

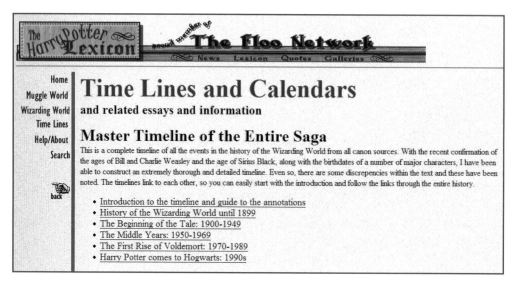

How to make a timeline

In this short workshop, we'll make a family timeline from scratch using the demo version of Progeny's Timeline Maker software. You can download this from **www.timelinemaker.com**. To unlock its full features will cost you $29.95.

When you first open the program, you will be in the Event Entry view. This is where you enter the information you want to include on your timeline. Start typing, adding dates as you go along.

Continue adding events. It is not necessary to enter it in chronological order as the software will sort it all out for you.

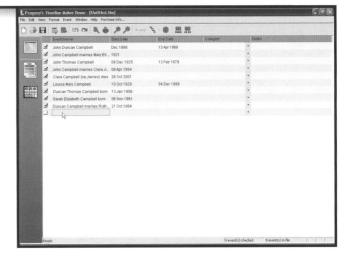

If you wish to remove an entry, simply click on the tick box to the left of the entry. The row will turn yellow. Then click on Entry in the top tool bar and then click on Delete Entry.

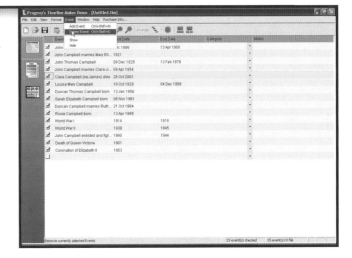

4

Once you have entered all your initial information, you can view the timeline by clicking on the timeline chart icon in the left-hand column.

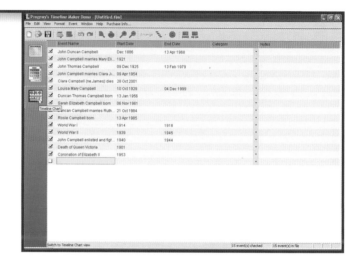

5

The first draft of your timeline will appear. If you want to add new entries now, click the Event Entry icon. This sits above the Timeline Chart icon in the left-hand column.

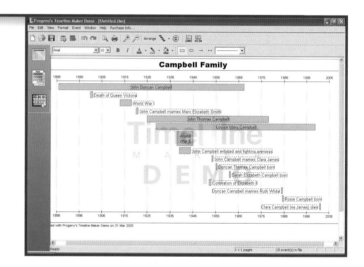

6

When you are happy with your timeline, you can alter the arrangement of the entries, add and change colours and fonts, and insert pictures. To change the colour of a bar, for example, click on the bar and select an alternative colour from the colour fill icon in the top toolbar.

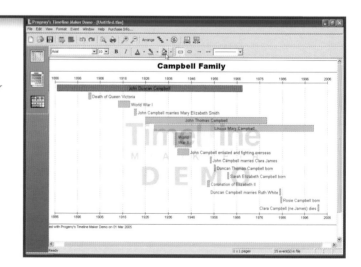

To change the font style and size, select the text and choose an alternative from the toolbar.

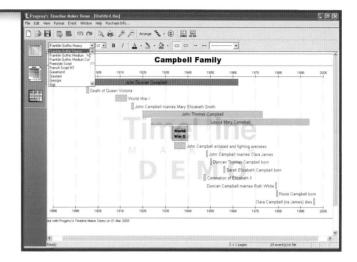

You can also insert photographs directly into your timeline by clicking Format, Insert picture and From File.

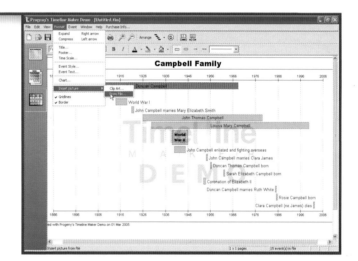

Once you have selected a picture, it appears within the timeline. You can now resize it by clicking on it to get a border and dragging it to the desired dimensions. You can also move the picture freely around the timeline.

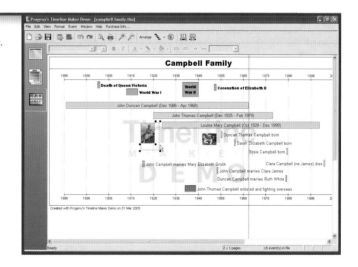

To edit any text in the timeline, double-click the relevant section. Up pops an edit window.

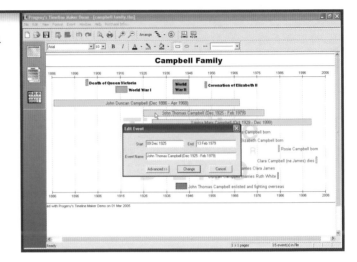

Once you are happy with your timeline, save it. The program creates a default folder called My Timelines but you could save it directly to your Genealogy folder if you prefer. Give your timeline a memorable name and then click save. You now have a document that can be printed or viewed by anyone else who has a copy of the program (but not otherwise).

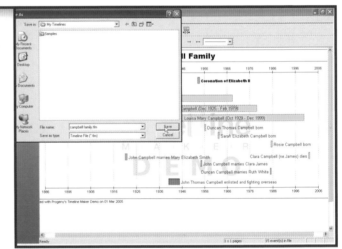

What you'll really want to do, of course, is publish the timeline directly on your family archive website. To do this, you need to save it as an HTML file. However, at this point you'll be asked to pay $29.95 to register the program.

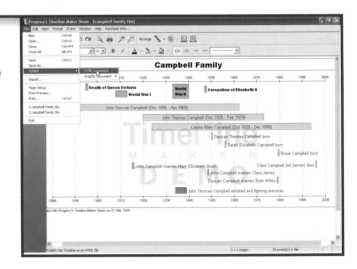

PART  **Make a map**

We mentioned maps earlier. In this workshop, we'll plot the movements of one Clara James using a Microsoft program called AutoRoute and save the results as a web page for inclusion in the archive (**www.microsoft.com/uk/homepc/autoroute**; £40 or less)

Open AutoRoute and you will be at the main map page. Move your arrow cursor to the area of the map you wish to focus on then click and drag to draw a box around it. For this example, we have selected the British Isles. Now click in the middle of your box to zoom in on your selected area.

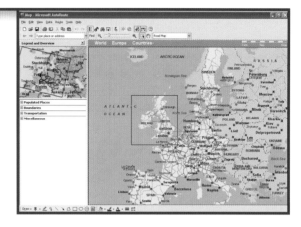

If your selected area is still too wide, click and draw another box and click in the middle to zoom again. You can also use the tool bar to zoom in and out by clicking the plus or minus icons.

You now need to find your first place of interest. To move around within your map, move the arrow cursor towards an edge until it changes into a larger white arrow. Left click, hold and move the mouse in the direction of the arrow. The map will scroll.

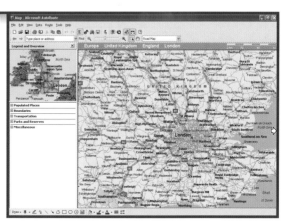

4

You can also click on the hand icon on the tool bar to click and drag the map around. Try zooming in and out with the mouse wheel if you have one.

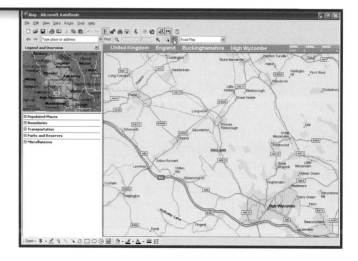

5

Alternatively, if you do not know where a place is or cannot find it on first inspection, click the Find icon. Make sure that the country box says United Kingdom (if not, click the arrow to get the dropdown list of countries). Now enter any address details you have: a full address, a postcode or a place name. Click Find.

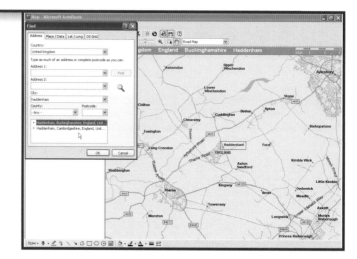

6

You will now see your location indicated on the map. To highlight it, click the pushpin icon on the toolbar at the bottom of the page, then move your curser to the map and left click on the location. A pushpin and a text box will appear.

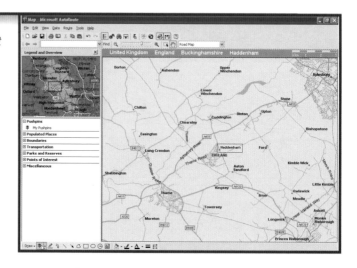

7

Enter some information into the text box. To remove a text box, click on the cross in the right-top corner of the box. To remove a pushpin, just click on it.

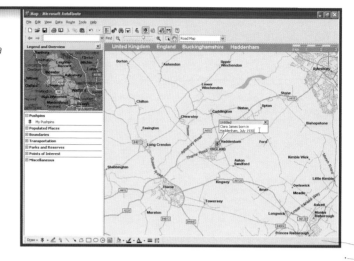

8

Continue to add and label pushpins at each location. Simply zoom out using the tool bar or the wheel on your mouse when you want see the entire map.

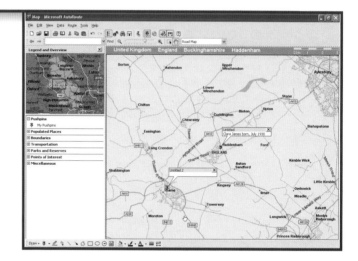

9

When you have finished, take a look at the finished map. You can edit text in any of the boxes simply by clicking in the box and retyping. If you have any overlapping text boxes, right-click on one and select Orientation. This allows you to reposition the text box.

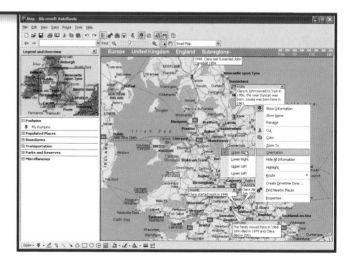

If you have a number of locations clustered together, making it difficult to display the information, you could create a second close-up map of that particular area. For example, Clara James was born in Haddenham and went to the local village school, and her grandmother also lived in the village. A close-up map could indicate all of these places.

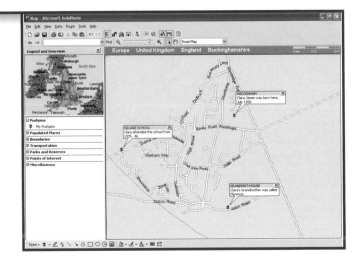

As well as pushpins, you can add other text boxes to your map. Select the text box icon on the bottom toolbar and click where you want a text box to appear. You can then type in your information and change the font colour or background colour using the tools on the bottom toolbar. This might be useful if you wanted to have some explanatory text on your map.

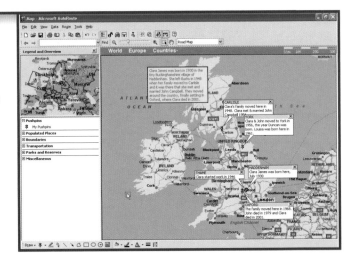

You can resize your map using the zoom buttons. Alternatively, click the Select icon on the top toolbar to activate the selection tool, then draw a box around the area of interest and double-click within it.

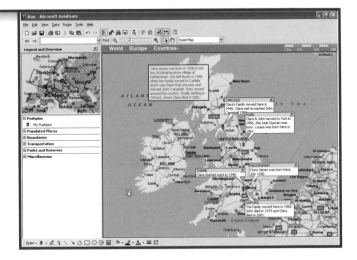

You now have a finished map ready for saving. Click File and then Save as Web Page.

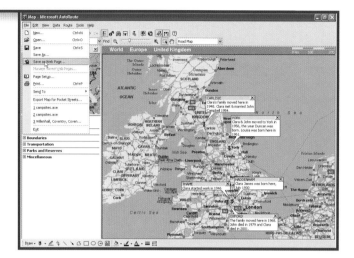

Give the map a title, uncheck both the map legend and map overview boxes, then browse to a suitable folder on your computer. Give your file a simple name with no spaces and click Save.

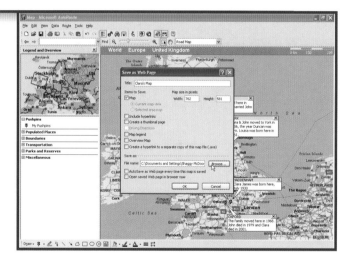

Close AutoRoute and open the folder where you have saved your map. You will see two items: a web page with the file name you chose and an associated folder. In this folder, you'll find the map as a simple image file (GIF format). You can now either use this image on any other web page in your family archive, or publish the AutoRoute file and folder together to make a self-contained web page. For more on publishing on the web, see Parts 5 and 7.

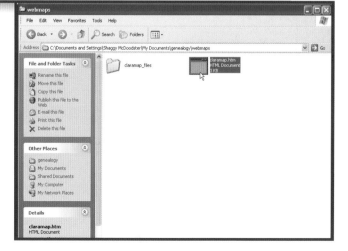

PART  # Interviewing relatives

Family memories are your best source of information. Do not put off asking elderly relatives about their lives and their memories. They may be your one and only source for the family stories that will really bring your research to life, and they won't be around forever.

What to ask?

As the fundamental tenet of any family tree is accuracy, it is crucial that the first thing you ask your relative to do is to confirm their own full name, date and place of birth, and details of any spouses and children. Once that is established you may want to go further and ask for the same information for his or her parents, grandparents and siblings.

It is very important to ascertain whether your relative has any original documents, photographs or other memorabilia that could assist you in your research. If you have any photographs of relatives that you cannot identify, take them along. You never know when an old photo of a once-familiar face (or car) will spark a memory and lead to new lines of research.

After that, it's up to you. What are you interested in for your family archive? Do you have an angle? A good rule of thumb is simply to ask questions that interest you. It may be that you are looking for information on one particular relative or want to ask questions about particular places or events in your family history. Or you may just want to know everything there is to know.

A good way to trigger memories is to take along a photograph and begin by asking about the people in it. Another way is to recall a known family event such as a wedding, and ask them about their recollection of it.

Ask a relative about significant events in their lives: about having to go to war and fight, perhaps, or what it was like living in Britain during the war, or seeing television for the first time, or buying their first car, or living through the coal miners' strikes. It is very important to gather accurate names and dates as well as more general memories, as this will help you to further your research. The World Wars are good examples of where the accuracy of the names of regiments or ships and the dates of postings overseas are crucial.

You could ask about the kinds of clothes they used to wear, what school used to be like, the toys they played with and the food they ate. You could ask them to describe the homes they lived in and what a typical day would have been like when they were young.

The results could be presented in your archive as a straight questions and answers document or summarised in flowing text as a journalistic interview.

Sometimes it doesn't take much to get an elderly relative reminiscing.

Here are some sample questions to ask a relative about a specific person, such as a grandmother:

What was her full name?

Did she have a nickname?

When and where was she born?

When and where did she die?

Was she buried or cremated?

Do you know the cause of death?

Was she married?

What was the date of the marriage?

Who did she marry?

Do you know how and where they met?

Did they have children?

What were their children's names and dates of birth?

Where did she live? Do you have any addresses for her?

Do you know what school she went to?

Do you know if she worked? What work did she do?

Do you have any photographs of her or any mementos or documents?

Can you suggest any other relatives who might be able to tell me more about her?

And here are some questions to ask grandfather about the war:

When did you join up?

What was your rank and the name of your regiment?

What was the name of your regiment's commander?

Who was your best friend?

Can you recall the full names of any of the other people in your regiment?

What was your job within the regiment?

Where did you go for training?

What was your uniform like?

When and where was your first overseas posting?

How long did you spend overseas?

What were the conditions like overseas?

Did you get letters and parcels from home?

How often were you allowed to go home on visits?

Did you ever get injured?

Did you get any medals?

When were you de-mobbed?

Do you have any particular memories of the war, good or bad, that you could share with the family?

Audio and video clips

As well as asking questions and writing down the answers, or perhaps instead of this, consider recording 'interviews' with your relatives. As well as reminiscing, perhaps they have a skill that they could demonstrate, like playing the spoons or making lace. Maybe there is a family christening dress or other items that they could produce from a cupboard, or a selection of family photographs that they can talk about while you film them. You'll probably end up taking a lot of footage and of course you won't use it all, but you just might capture a truly priceless 30 second clip of Grandma reminiscing fondly about Grandad. So long as she agrees, this would make a valuable addition to your online archive.

If there are old family home movies, transfer them to your computer in digital form and seek out the best bits. You might be able to stitch together a short film that shows the passing of time: people getting older, babies arriving, clothing changing, cars getting smaller and more up to date. As ever, this will make a welcome addition to your archive.

See Appendices 1 and 2 for more on working with audio and video.

Get the whole family involved for a relaxed video project.

PART  Getting the children involved

Helping to assemble the family tree is a great way for children to learn more about their ancestors and to get a real appreciation of where they come from. It will help them to understand all the family relationships, such as what it means when Bob is described as their second cousin. Involvement can help to bridge the gap between young and old and develop a strong sense of family, whilst also enabling you to undertake a shared activity.

A little perspective

Crucially, it helps children understand how different their lives are today to people living, say, 50 years ago (before TV and fast food were invented). They will be amazed at how the world has changed in such a short space of time.

It can also help develop an appreciation for 'dry' school subjects like history and geography. History comes to life when they understand that it's really the study of how people lived, and all the more so when they can relate 'people' to somebody they know or have heard about. Geography takes on a new meaning when maps are used to pinpoint where their ancestors came from.

Children also tend to have good IT skills and a real enthusiasm for using the computer so they can help with inputting data, scanning documents and photos, and doing research online.

Projects for children

Here are some suggestions for getting the kids onboard:
- Collect family photographs and scan them so that they can be added to the online family tree.
- Find a photo with a story behind it and encourage the child to ask questions.
- Interview your grandparents or other elderly relatives to find out what their childhoods and school days were like. Use email if they live far away (or, of course, exchange letters). Type up the

Was dad a demonstrator? The story must be told!

Children should be taught that future historians will one day be interested in where and when they went to school, and what it was like.

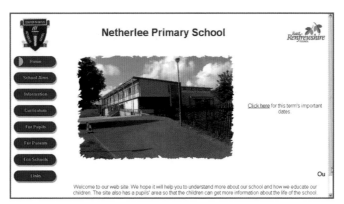

83

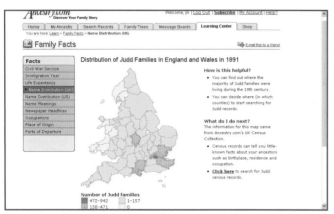

A search on Google can bring up all sorts of interesting things, such as this map showing the distribution of Judd families in England and Wales in 1891.

Then and now. Capture the passing of time with photographs of similar events.

interview and attach it to the family tree or archive. Better still, record it or film your chat and publish the clips online along with a transcription.

● Write a piece about your school days and lifestyle to attach to the family tree for future generations to read. Include photographs of your school and school friends, and, perhaps, a timetable of lessons. If the school has a website, include a link.

● Plot all the towns and countries where your ancestors were born on a map, and include a sentence or so about each place. This can then be scanned and added to the tree.

● Trace the origins of family surnames and forenames. What does your surname mean? Have certain forenames been passed down through the generations? How many family members share the same names? Does anyone else in the family tree have the same name as you?

● Put together an online photo album of the family by scanning existing old photographs and taking new digital photos. Then

give them funny captions and upload them to the family archive website. With portraits, see if you can spot any family characteristics – funny noses, the same colour of hair or eyes. Who do you look like? Consider grouping similar faces together or having a separate page for each generation or each family.

● Create a timeline for your own life that includes the major events that have happened to you. This might include learning to walk, learning to ride a bike, moving house, the birth of a sibling, and your first pet. Attach photographs of yourself at different ages, plus photos of your pets, toys, etc.

● Ask relatives what their favourite food was in their childhood and compile a 'family recipe book'. You can search for recipes online or get your relative to give you the recipe if they have it. Use any word processor to design a basic template for your cookbook and search for some free clipart to jazz it up a bit. Why not try cooking some of the foods, taking a photo of your efforts, and putting a review on the website?

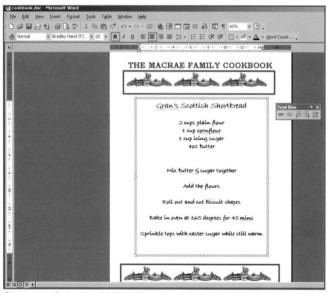

Share your favourite shortbread recipe with family far and wide.

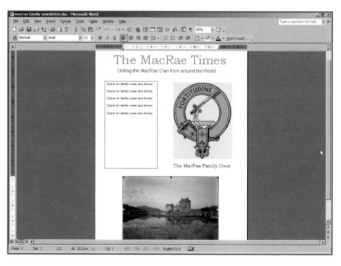

A simple newsletter can be designed in Word using the text box tool. Draw your text boxes anywhere you like on the page and then copy and paste text and images into them.

MY FAMILY TREE

TOM
Grandfather

JOHN
Grandfather

FIONA
Grandmother

LOUISE
Grandmother

ROBERT
Father

CLARE
Mother

Brother/Sister

Brother/Sister

KATY
Brother/Sister

Brother/Sister

TOM
ME

Brother/Sister

Walt Disney PICTURES PRESENTS
THE Tigger MOVIE

A simple family tree helps young
minds get a grip on who they are
and where they came from.

- Create an online family newspaper full of stories about different members of the family, both alive and dead. Perhaps write a piece about the oldest and the youngest family members. You can give your newspaper a name, like *The MacRae Times* or *Crick Family Chronicle*. Add photographs, include an events calendar that details what all the relatives are going to be up to over the next month or year, and keep track of births and marriages, graduations and parties. Ask relatives to email you when they have been up to something interesting then add it to the newspaper. And, of course, publish the newspaper online in your family archive.
- For the very young there are some online family tree templates that can be printed and filled in by hand. Take a look at **www.disney.go.com/disneyvideos/animatedfilms/tiggermovie/ familytree.html.**

Interview the oldies

Children should be encouraged to ask elderly relatives about their experiences. In fact, they may be better at extracting information than you! Here are some sample questions to use as the basis of an informal questionnaire:

Home Life
What was the home like where you were born and grew up?

How was it heated and lit?

Did you have a bathroom?

Daily Life
Did your Mum and Dad work?

What did they do?

Where did your food come from –
the garden or the shops?

How did you wash clothes?

How often did you have to
have a bath?

Where did you get your hair cut?

Did you have to do chores?

Clothing
What kind of clothes did you wear?

Did you have clothes for best?

What were your shoes like?

School
What age were you when you
started and finished school?

Where was your school and how did you get there each day?

Did you wear a uniform?

Did you eat school lunch? What was it like?

Was it very strict at your school?

Leisure Time
What were your favourite games, sports and toys?

Did you listen to music, the radio or watch TV at home?

Did you go to the cinema?

Did you have family holidays? Where did you go?

Did you have a car?

PART 5 INTERNET GENEALOGY MANUAL
Preparing for the web

PART 5 A crash-course in web design

Having collected sufficient raw data to start a family tree and hopefully having compiled a bunch of scans, photographs and video clips to turn it into a full-blown family archive, it's time to start thinking about how best to turn all this information into something usable and share it on the internet.

What we need here is a basic understanding of the web, for that's where your archive will 'live'. Don't panic if this is all completely new to you, for there's really nothing much to it. However, it is worth getting to grips with the absolute basics just so you know how to fix things if they go wrong.

What do we mean by the web?

When people talk about the internet, they often mean the World Wide Web – but they're not the same thing. The internet is the giant computer network that takes care of delivering our emails, transferring files and so on, and the web sits on top of that network. Essentially, the internet is the plumbing that makes the web work.

The web is a giant library, but instead of books it has sites. For example, the BBC website has pages about particular TV programmes, about radio shows, about videos and so on. What makes the web so special – and so useful – is that pages link to one another. If you're on the BBC home page, you can click 'Radio' and you'll be taken to the radio page.

You can do exactly the same thing with your family history if you publish it online. For example, you could have a page that shows the entire family tree and then individual pages about each member of your family. Clicking on your name would display the page about you; clicking on Gran's name would display the page about Gran; and the whole site would be available to anyone, anywhere in the world. You're not just limited to text, either: your site can include pictures, photos, sounds and even video clips. Best of all, it's really easy to do, as we'll discover over the next few pages.

Hooray for hyperlinks

Hyperlinks, or links, are the bits of a web page you click to make something happen. They often appear in blue writing with an underline. If you visit the BBC home page, you'll see dozens of links; in fact, the entire page is made of links. Each link takes you to a particular page, so clicking on 'History' takes you to the BBC's history page, clicking on 'Entertainment' takes you to the entertainment page, and so on.

So how do hyperlinks work? They have two sections: the bit you see and the bit your web browser sees. For example, on the BBC home page there's a link that says 'Radio 1'; if you click it, you'll be taken to the Radio 1 page. However, the link also

Affordable products like Microsoft FrontPage make it easy for anybody to design and publish a website.

contains a crucial bit of information for your web browser: the actual address of the page. You see 'Radio 1', but your browser sees **http://www.bbc.co.uk/radio1**; you see 'Family History', but your browser sees **http://www.bbc.co.uk/history/familyhistory**. Don't worry about the **http://** prefix, as this is simply a bit of code that tells your web browser to look on the internet rather than on your computer.

These addresses are like driving directions, but instead of saying 'go down the high street, past the chip shop and turn left at the lights' they tell your web browser how to find a page. For example, when you click the BBC's 'Family History' link, the hyperlink says to your browser, 'Go to the BBC site and you'll see a folder called "history". Open that folder and you'll see another folder inside it, called "familyhistory". That's the one you want.'

How websites work

A website is simply a collection of files – pages, photos, video clips and so on – stored on a computer. In fact, it's almost identical to a folder on your PC. For example, you'll probably store your documents in your computer's My Documents folder and you might have created additional folders to further organise your stuff: a folder for personal letters, another one for the family budget, and so on. Within those folders, you'll have your files, each of which will have a unique name.

Websites work in exactly the same way. Sites can contain folders for specific things, so for example the BBC website has a folder called Radio, which in turn contains folders for Radio 1, Radio 2 and so on. Each of those folders contains files – the pages, sound clips and photographs that you see on screen – and each of those files has a unique name. The combination of that file name, the site it's on and the folder it lives in is the internet address of each file.

Understanding addresses

In order to find a file, you need to know where it is. On your computer, it's likely that your documents live in the My Documents folder on your hard disk, while your photos will be in My Pictures. If you have lots of files, it's a good idea to organise these folders further with sub-folders.

Let's say you have a folder in My Pictures called Christmas, and there's a particular image in that folder called Gran. Its address *on your computer* would be something like this:

C:\My Pictures\Christmas\Gran.jpg

The first bit – C: – is your hard disk, and the rest of the address is like driving directions: open up the C drive, go to My Pictures, look in the Christmas folder and find the file called Gran. The '.jpg' at the end means the file is a JPEG image, which is the kind of file created by most digital cameras.

If the same file were *on the internet*, its address wouldn't be dramatically different. If a web page were to link to the photo of your Gran it would use an address something like this:

www.mysite.co.uk/pictures/christmas/gran.jpg

Links are usually – but not always – displayed in blue, underlined text. The easiest way to spot a link is to move your mouse over it. If it's a link, the mouse pointer becomes a pointing finger.

Websites are organised into folders. For example, this page is in the folder called 'DJs', which in turn is in the 'radio1' folder of the BBC website.

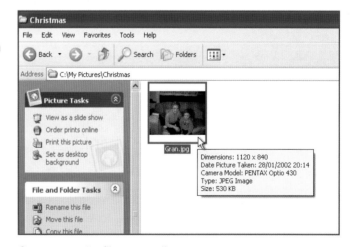

On your computer, files are usually stored within folders within folders. The 'path', or address, is expressed with backslashes that separate one folder from the next.

89

internet addresses are simple things: the 'www' tells your browser that the site is on the web, and the remaining bit is a domain name – in this case, Google's UK site.

As you can see, we still have the directions – open the Pictures folder, look for the sub-folder called Christmas, and find the image file called Gran – but the bit at the beginning is slightly different. The bit that says **www.mysite.co.uk** is the website address. It follows a simple formula.

The first part of the address – **www** – tells your web browser that the site you're looking for is on the web. The rest of the site address is called a domain name, in this case **mysite.co.uk**. It's possible to buy a domain name for pennies so, for example, you could have **www.juddfamilyarchive.co.uk**. We'll look at that in more detail in just a moment.

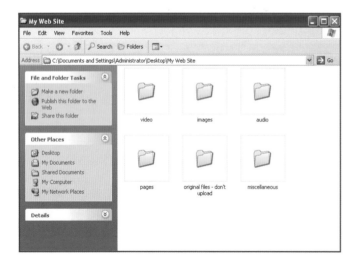

It's a very good idea to organise your website into different folders: that way, it's easy to find your files. Use the same folder names on your computer as you'll use in your website.

Think local

Web browsers are very picky. If a link says **www.mysite.co.uk/pictures/christmas/gran.jpg** but the file is actually at **www.mysite.co.uk/pictures/christmas05/gran.jpg**, then the browser won't display the file; instead, it'll go in a huff and tell you that the page can't be found. To prevent this from happening, it's important to test any site thoroughly before you stick it on the internet.

The simplest way to make a site that works is to have a sensible, organised structure on your hard disk and to use the same structure for your website. For example, on your computer you might create a folder called My website and then have sub-folders called Images, Audio and Video. When you put your site on the internet, those folders would become:

> **www.mysite.co.uk/images**
> **www.mysite.co.uk/audio**
> **www.mysite.co.uk/video**

Taking the example of the Christmas picture, you might store it on your computer like this:

C:\my website\images\christmas\gran.jpg

On your website, it'd be here:

www.mysite.co.uk/images/christmas/gran.jpg

If you have the same folders on your hard disk that you intend to have on your website, it makes life much easier, as you can build your site and check everything works before unveiling it to the rest of the world.

It's very important to think about the structure of your site before you start building it, because it's difficult to make big changes to a site when you've already started putting pages together. The best thing to do is to sit down with a cup of tea and a bit of paper, and sketch out the structure you think will work best for your site. In the case of our family album, you might have folders for different kinds of things – for example, a folder where you keep images, or a folder where you keep video – or you might want to use a different folder for each family member. It's entirely up to you.

PART **5**

Hosts with the most

The next step is to decide where you're going to put your website. On the internet, obviously, but for that you need some web space.

There are three main options:
- If the internet package from your internet Service Provider (ISP) includes web space, you could use that.
- You could sign up for free web space from a service such as Tripod.
- You could buy web space from a professional hosting firm.

There are pros and cons to each approach.

Web space from your ISP

Many ISPs give their customers free web space and lots of help pages that explain how to use it. At the time of writing, customers of BT Yahoo's cheapest package get 15MB of space thrown in. The obvious benefit is that such space is free, but there's not much of it, particularly if you want to use video clips, which can be massive. The site address is likely to be rubbish, too; you might get something like this: **www.myisp.com/webspace/users/33322424/site**.

15MB of free web space from BT Yahoo.

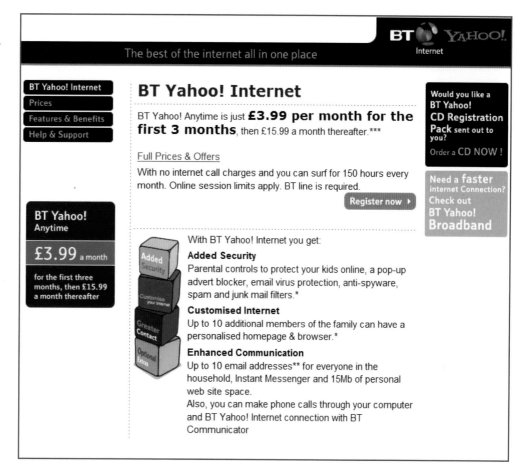

Free web space

Companies such as Tripod (**www.tripod.lycos.co.uk**) offer free
web space that anybody can sign up for, and the offers are
generous: with Tripod you get a massive 50MB of web space
plus lots of free tools such as guestbooks and other site goodies.
However, there's no such thing as a free lunch: if you use free
web space, your site will display banner adverts and possibly
pop-up adverts too, and if your site proves too popular the host
might temporarily disable it. You'll get a slightly more
comprehensible web address than if you use your ISP's free web
space, but it'll still be a little clunky: expect to get an address
such as **www.members.tripod.com/juddfamilyarchive**.

Space from a web hosting firm

The biggest advantage of space from a web hosting firm is that
it's advertising-free, so you don't need to worry about your pages
being used to hawk products. It's reasonably cheap, too: 1&1
internet (**www.oneandone.co.uk)** offers a basic package called
Instant Website for £1.99 per month. This gives you 250MB of
web space to play with and also includes some extra features
such as email accounts (with anti-virus and spam filtering) and
24-hour technical support. In many cases, if you buy space from
a web hosting firm you'll also get a domain name – such as
juddfamilyarchive.co.uk – as part of the package.

   As you can see, there are ups and downs. Free web space
from your ISP or from a firm such as Tripod is a good way to
explore basic web design, but you don't get a great web address
and there may be limits to what you can do. In the case of free
web space providers, there's also the problem of adverts: not
everyone wants ads on their site, and your visitors might not
appreciate them either. If you've got a bit of spare cash, buying
space from a hosting firm is probably the best bet: you get loads
of space, lots of support and plenty of tools to help you manage
your site and discover where your visitors come from.

Companies such as Tripod will
happily give you lots of web space
for free, but in return they'll put
advertising on your carefully
crafted pages.

Domain games

Whichever form of web hosting you go for, you should consider buying a domain name. A domain is a website name like **juddfamilyarchive.co.uk**. There are several reasons for doing this:

- It replaces your web space's rather clunky address with something more memorable.
- It can be used to give you email addresses such as **dad@juddfamilyarchive.co.uk**.
- It's cheap: you can get a domain name for as little as £1.99 for two years.

When you buy a domain name from a site such as 123reg (**www.123reg.co.uk**), it comes with a control panel. This is a web page that enables you to control how your domain name works. For example, you could use the control panel to set up an email address called **dad@juddfamilyarchive.co.uk** and redirect incoming mail to your normal email address. This way, any time anyone sends a message to the juddfamilyarchive email address, the message is automatically redirected to your email inbox. It's the electronic equivalent of a Post Office redirect.

The other thing your control panel enables you to do is to make your domain name point to a website regardless of where it is hosted on the internet. Let's say your site is hosted on your ISP's free web space, and its true address is something like this:

www.myisp.co.uk/webpages/users/mr_judd

And you have folders organised like this:

www.myisp.co.uk/webpages/users/mr_judd/video
www.myisp.co.uk/webpages/users/mr_judd/audio
www.myisp.co.uk/webpages/users/mr_judd/photos

Using your control panel, you could get **www.juddfamilyarchive.co.uk** to point to that web space. As a result, your folders would have the following internet addresses:

www.juddfamilyarchive.co.uk/video
www.juddfamilyarchive.co.uk/audio
www.juddfamilyarchive.co.uk/photos

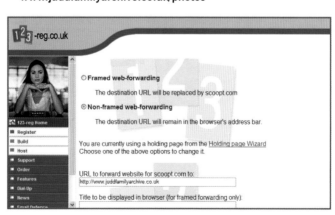

A domain name control panel allows you to redirect one web address to another.

Final thoughts

When you're considering a domain name, it's important to know two things. First of all, a domain name isn't a permanent purchase: when you buy a name, you get it for two years and you have to renew it every two years. This is an automatic process – the firm who sold you the name will email you when it's time to renew it, and it's just a matter of paying the £1.99 for the next two years – but if you don't renew the name then you'll lose it and it will no longer work. It's possible that if you don't renew the name, someone else might buy it. This could be embarrassing if your friends or family use the address and discover that it now points to something dodgy.

The second thing you need to know is that there are different kinds of domain. The cheapest and most popular one for UK users is a **.co.uk** address, such as **juddfamilyarchive.co.uk**. The **.co.uk** bit means it's a British site. However, you'll also see other kinds of addresses advertised, such as **.com** (which tends to be used by companies), **.org** (for charities and voluntary groups) and so on. We'd stick with the **.co.uk** option.

So you've decided on the folder structure of your site, you've decided where you're going to put it and you've chosen your domain name. The next step is to start putting your site together. Over the next few pages, we'll find out how to do just that.

Companies such as 123reg will happily sell you a .co.uk address for a few pounds. Don't let the headline figures fool you, though: the 9p in our screenshot doesn't include a £2.50 admin fee.

PART  # Register a domain name

Although it's quite possible (and sometimes cheaper) to buy your domain name from one company and your web space from another, it does involve quite a bit of hassle. Buying them as a package is much easier. You'll find that if you buy web space from a firm such as 1&1 internet (**www.oneandone.co.uk**), you'll get a free domain name as part of the package. In this workshop we'll take you step by step through the process of buying web space and registering a domain from 1&1. It only takes a few minutes and doesn't cost a fortune.

Buying a domain name and web space is as simple as any other kind of online shopping. To choose a suitable package, open your web browser and type **www.oneandone.co.uk** *in the address bar. When the page loads you'll see an ad displaying the firm's latest special offer. Click this to go to the site's main page.*

Click the Instant Website link at the left of the screen and you'll see this page telling you about all the goodies that come with the Instant Website package. The most attractive feature is its price: just £1.99 per month and you get a domain name for free. Click Sign Up to begin the registration process.

3

When you click Sign Up, the site will confirm your selection. If you want to go for a different package, clicking on Select a Different Package will take you back to the products page. If you're happy with your choice, click the Continue button.

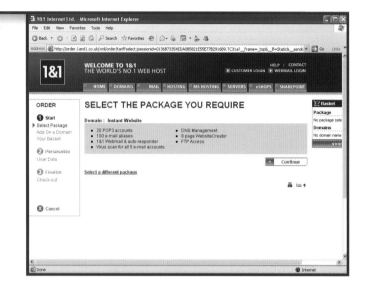

4

Now you need to tell 1&1 what domain name you'd like to use. Enter this in the box at the bottom of the screen (don't bother with the **http://www**. bit). In this example, we'll enter **juddfamilyarchive.co.uk**. Click Check Domain and after a few seconds, the site will tell you if the domain name is available.

5

If your chosen domain name is available to register, 1&1 will show it at the top of the page and will automatically select its tick box. It'll also display some alternatives, such as **juddfamilyarchive.com**. You can buy additional addresses if you wish, but we think they're an unnecessary expense: a single **.co.uk** domain name is all you need. Click Continue to proceed.

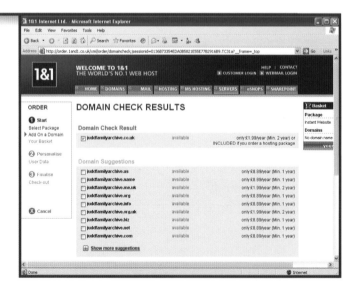

1&1 will now display your shopping basket, and as you'll notice the price seems to have increased from £1.99 per month. That's because 1&1 bills you once per year, so the figures you see here are the total costs for 12 months. Have a read through the small print at the bottom of the page and then click Continue when you're ready to proceed.

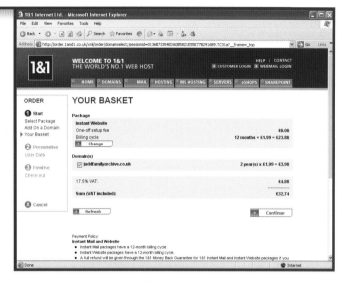

The next step is to provide 1&1 with your contact details: your home address, contact telephone number and most importantly of all, your email address. Once you've ordered your domain and web space all the details will be sent to this address, so it's important to make sure you don't misspell it. Click Continue when you've entered the appropriate information.

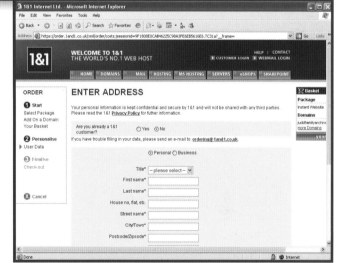

By default, your personal details will be available for other people to see using a thing called a WHOIS search. This enables people to search for a particular domain and find out who owns it. If you'd rather not be included in the WHOIS database – the internet equivalent of going ex-directory – you'll need to un-tick the box at the bottom of the page before clicking on Continue.

9

The next step is to choose a password, which you'll use whenever you want to log in to your web space. The password needs to be between 6 and 18 characters, and you shouldn't use anything that's easy for other people to guess. Type your password in both boxes and then click Continue.

10

Although it's hardly an essential part of registering a domain, 1&1 likes to know whether its advertising is effective, and as a result it asks you how you found out about the site. Sadly, there isn't an option that says 'from the Haynes Internet Genealogy book', so choose any option at all before clicking on Continue.

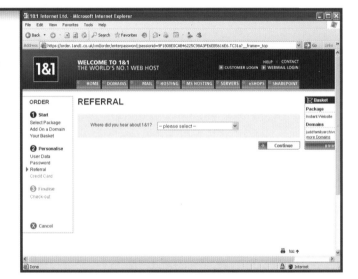

11

It's time to reach for your wallet, for the site prompts you to enter your card details before you can continue. You can use Switch, Delta, Visa or MasterCard, and you'll be asked to provide your Card Verification Code. This is a code printed on the signature strip on the back of your card; the Verification Code is the last three digits.

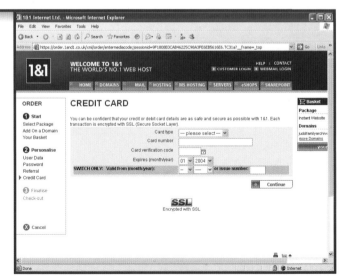

Before clicking Continue, look at the bottom right-hand corner of your browser window. There should be a little golden padlock immediately to the left of the 'internet' message. This padlock tells you that you're on a secure website, and means that when you enter any card details the site will scramble them so that they can't fall into the wrong hands. You should never enter card details into a site that isn't secure.

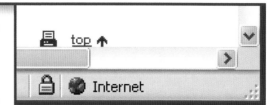

The final screen is just like any other online shop: it tells you exactly what you're about to order and repeats the user information and card details you've provided. Make sure you haven't made any little mistakes, such as a typing error in your domain name, because once you click the Place Order button you can't go back and change any of the details. When you're happy with the checkout page, click Place Order.

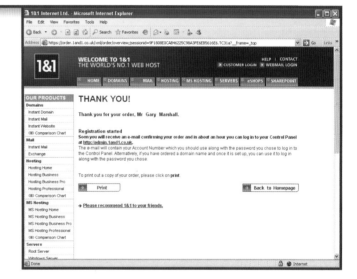

Congratulations! You are now the proud owner of a domain name and a big chunk of web space. You won't be able to use it immediately, though: 1&1 will send you an email confirming your purchase and letting you know the username and password you'll need to access your site. The email usually takes an hour or so to arrive. As soon as it turns up, you're ready to start building your site.

PART  **Exploring your new site**

The computer that stores your website is called a web server because it 'serves' up pages to your site visitors. The good news is that organising a server is no more difficult than organising your hard disk. In this workshop we'll discover how you can take a look at your web space and how to create folders. Once we've done that, we're ready to start building a website.

1

You'll receive an email from 1&1 confirming that your new account has been set up. Take a note of the account number, open your web browser and visit **admin.oneandone.co.uk** *(with no* **www.** *before it). Enter your account number in the first field and the password you selected when you purchased your web space in the second.*

2

After a few seconds you'll be presented with a screen which displays your websites. As we only bought one site, there's just one entry in the list. Click either the Instant Website link in the middle of the screen or the Administration button to go to the next screen.

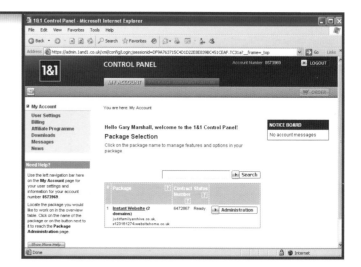

This screen gives you quick access to common tasks such as changing your billing details, setting up email accounts and so on. For now, we'll ignore those options and choose the Web Space/Access link. This will give us the information we need to explore our new site.

You'll now be presented with two options: Webspace Explorer and FTP Account. Although Webspace Explorer is designed to help you navigate your website it's rather slow and we'll use a different method. To do this, we need the File Transfer Protocol (FTP) details. Click FTP Account to see them.

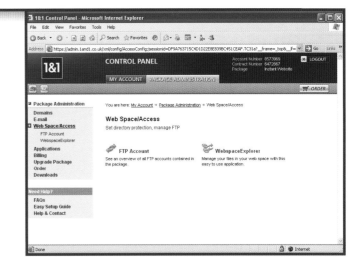

You'll now see a user name and password. Print out this screen or take a note of the information, as we'll need these details in this workshop and in the next one too. If you want to change your FTP password, you can do so by clicking on the username and then entering a new password, but the default passwords are hard to guess so you don't need to change them if you don't want to.

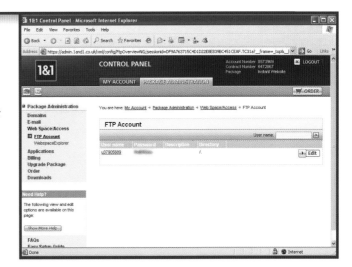

In Internet Explorer's address bar, enter
ftp.juddfamilyarchive.co.uk (replace juddfamilyarchive with your
domain name). This tells Internet Explorer that you want to take
a look at your website, but you want to use FTP instead of the
usual web browser. Don't worry too much about the term FTP –
it's much simpler than it sounds.

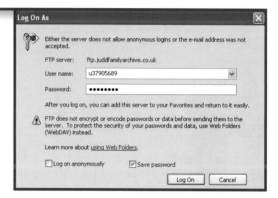

The first time you attempt to access your site by FTP, Internet
Explorer will ask you for your username and password. Enter the
details you copied from the 1&1 Control Panel and then make
sure the Save Password box is ticked (unless you're using
someone else's computer and don't want to store passwords on
it). This means you won't have to type in the username and
password on every visit.

And here's your website. When it's first created there are only
two things in it: a file called index.html, which is a holding page
that visitors will see if you don't upload pages of your own, and a
folder called Logs, which stores reports such as visitor logs. You
can access these reports through your 1&1 Control Panel.

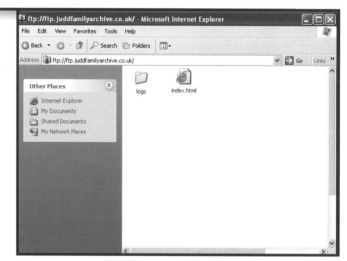

Creating a new folder on your website is as easy as creating new
folders on your hard disk: simply right-click in the Internet
Explorer window and then choose New > Folder. We want to
create several folders: one for images, one for audio, one for
video and one for miscellaneous bits and bobs.

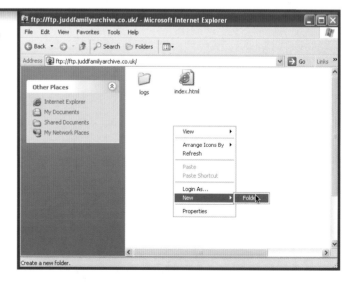

A new folder should now appear in the same window as the Logs folder and the index.html file; to rename it, simply type its new name – in this case, 'audio' (without the inverted commas) – and then click away from the folder. Repeat the process to create new folders called 'images', 'miscellaneous' and 'video'.

When you've created the folders, the result should look something like this. Browsing folders works in exactly the same way as browsing folders on your hard disk. If you want to rename or delete a folder, simply right-click it and choose the appropriate option. Once you're happy with your folders, close the window: it's time to put some web pages together.

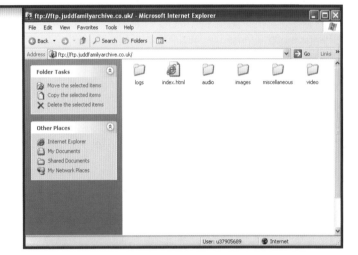

Mini trouble-shooter

If you encounter problems when you try to connect to your website via FTP, there are two things to check. In Internet Explorer, go to Tools > Internet Options > Advanced and scroll down until you see an option called 'Enable folder view for FTP sites'. If this box isn't ticked, tick it and then click OK. That's usually the culprit.

If Internet Explorer is configured correctly and you still don't have any joy connecting, check the settings on any firewall software you may have installed on your PC. Firewalls can be over-protective sometimes and your firewall may be blocking your attempts to connect via FTP.

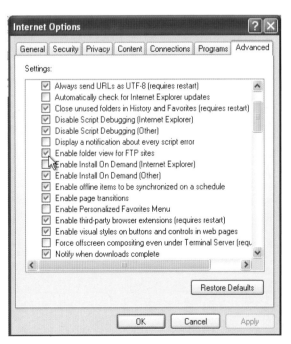

Enable folder view for FTP sites to use Internet Explorer to upload files to your website.

PART 5 Creating your first web pages

You've registered a domain name, splashed out on some web space and created some folders on your shiny new server, so the next step is to actually put some pages together. There are lots of page building programs to choose from, but we'd recommend Nvu (**www.nvu.com**) for three good reasons: it's brilliant; it's easy to use; and it doesn't cost a penny. As you'll discover in this workshop, creating web pages isn't much more complicated than creating normal pages in a word processor.

You'll need to download and install Nvu before starting this workshop and you'll need the same FTP account details you used on p102.

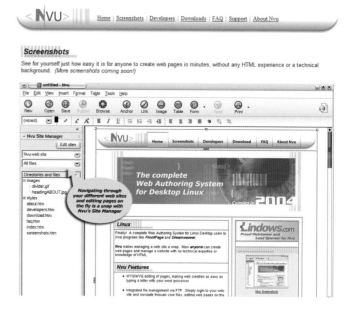

A fully-featured and completely free what-you-see-is-what-you-get web editor from Nvu.

Before we can start creating pages, we need to create some folders to put everything in. It's important that we have the same structure on our computer as we have on our website. Right-click the Windows Desktop and select New > Folder to create a new folder on the desktop.

A new folder called New Folder should now appear on your desktop. Type a more descriptive name for the folder – it doesn't matter what name you go for, but something like My website isn't a bad idea. Double-click the folder when you've given it a name.

Inside this folder, create subfolders for the different kinds of files you'll be using in your site – audio, images, video and miscellaneous – by again using the right-click menu and selecting New > Folder. As you'd expect, we'll store image files in the images folder, audio files in the audio folder and so on.

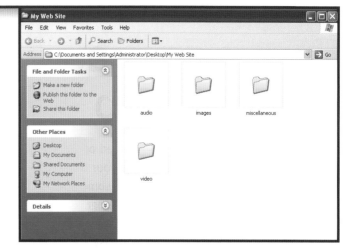

For this workshop we'll be using an image. It doesn't matter what image you use, but it's important that you copy it to the My website > Images folder before you start building web pages. In this example we've dug up an old photo of Gramps, called gramps.jpg.

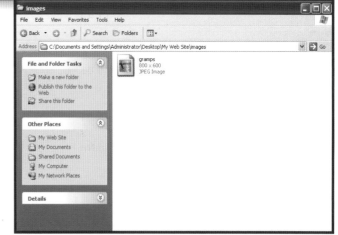

Open the Nvu program. The first time you run it, you'll see a tips window in the middle of the screen; if you don't want this window to appear every time you run Nvu, uncheck the 'Show Tips at Startup' box. Click Close to get rid of the tips window for now.

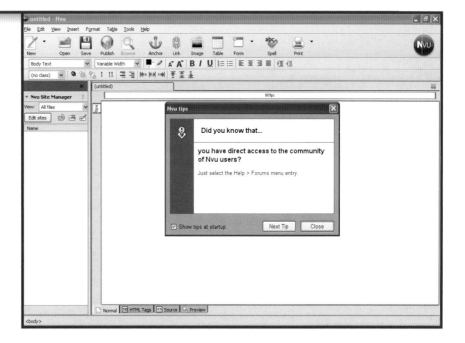

In the main window, type in the text you'd like to use in your test page. As you can see, it's just like using a word processor. You can type whatever you want, but finish with 'Click here to see a picture'. That's the text we'll be using to create our first hyperlink.

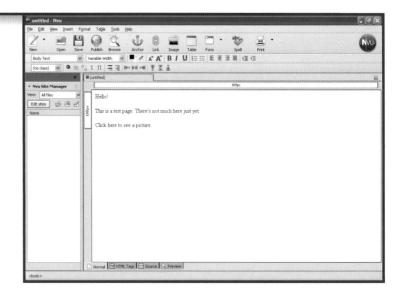

Before we can create a link, we need another page to link to. Go to the File menu and select New. Make sure that 'A blank document' is selected and then click Create. Nvu will now create a second blank web page and open it in the main window.

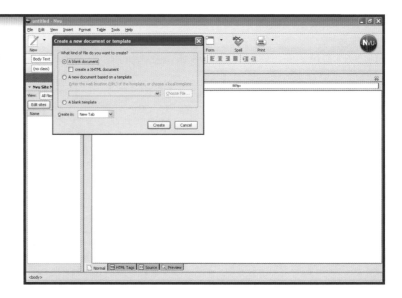

This page will contain a photograph, but it also needs some text; at the top of the page, type a quick bit of descriptive text and then press the return key a few times. Once you've done that, you're almost ready to add an image. First, though, you need to save the file. Click File > Save As.

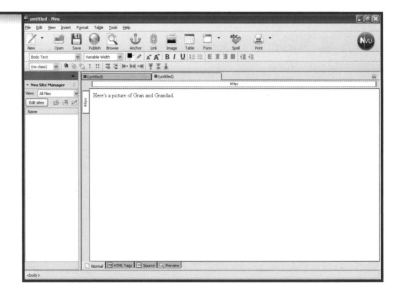

When you save a page, Nvu first asks you to give the page a title. This isn't the filename; the page title is the text that appears at the very top of your visitors' web browsers, and it's the headline you'll see when your site is listed in search engine results. Type a meaningful title and then click OK.

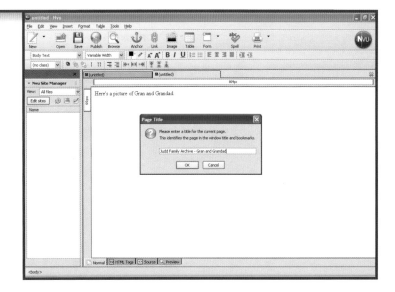

Nvu will now ask you for a filename and location. In the File Name box, enter 'test2.htm' (without the inverted commas) and make sure you save the file in the My website folder. If you save the file anywhere else, the test site won't work.

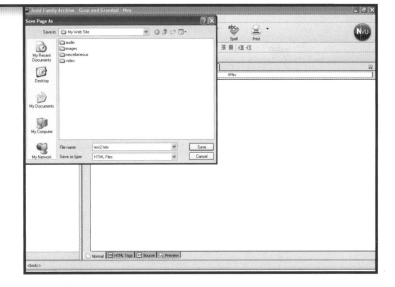

Nvu will take you back to the main editing window. Click the Image icon in the toolbar to add an image. Use the Choose File button to open the Browse window, navigate to My website > Images and click your image file. Make sure that the 'URL is relative to page location' box is checked, and add some descriptive text in the 'Alternate Text' field: this will appear if your visitors have chosen not to view images in their browsers.

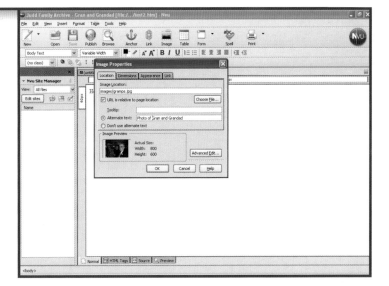

If everything's working properly, your photograph should now appear just underneath the descriptive text you added earlier. If the image is a bit too big, click it and dots will appear at each corner; drag the dots to make the image smaller. Once you're happy with the image size, choose File > Save.

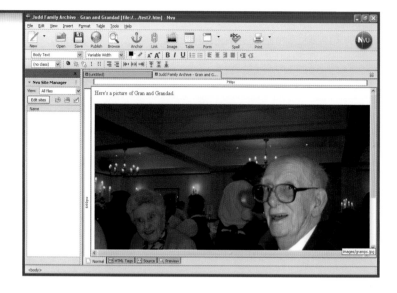

You'll see two tabs just above the main window. These are your open files, so (untitled) is the first test page you created. The second tab should contain the title of your second page. We need to make some more changes to our first test page, so click the (untitled) tab to return to that page.

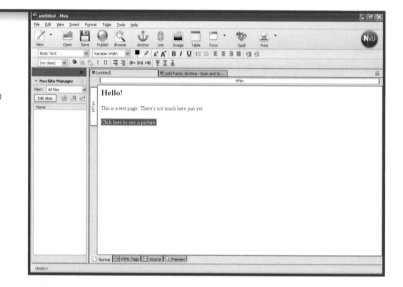

Before you can add a link, you need to save your page. Click File > Save As and, once again, you'll be asked to give your page a title. Don't use the same title as your other page or things will get very confusing! When you've entered a title, click OK to continue. Save the file as test.htm in your My website folder.

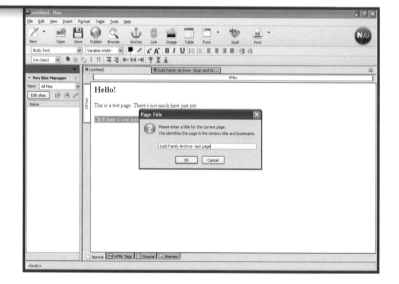

It's time to add a hyperlink. Highlight the 'Click here to see a picture' text and then click the Link icon in the toolbar. In the Link Location field, type 'test2.htm' (without the inverted commas) or use the Choose File button to locate the test2.htm file. Click OK when you've done this.

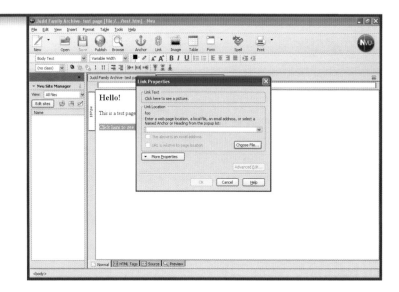

Congratulations – you've successfully created your very first hyperlink. Now we'll upload your masterpiece to the web. To do this, we'll use Nvu's built-in Site Manager. To the left of the editing window you'll see a section headed Nvu Site Manager. Click the Edit Sites button.

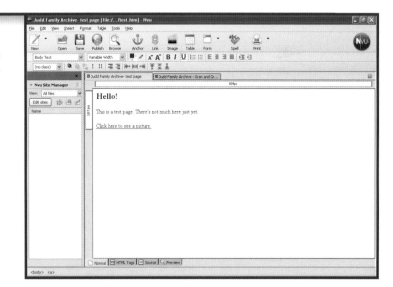

Remember the FTP login information you printed off in Step 5 on p101? You'll need those details again. Nvu needs to know the FTP address, user name and password of your website. Enter this information in the appropriate fields, tick the 'Save Password' box, and then click OK. Nvu will take you back to the main editing window.

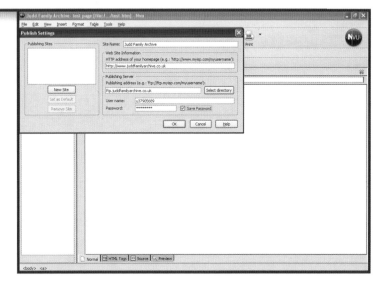

In the test.htm page, click the Save icon and then click File > Publish As. This brings up the Publish dialog box. You don't need to change any of these details. Make sure you're connected to the internet and then click the Publish button to upload your page.

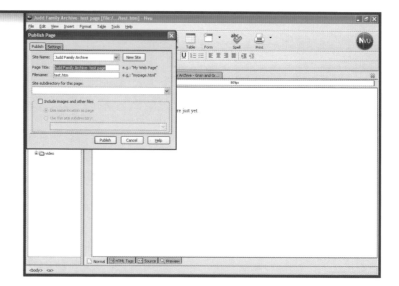

After a few seconds, the Publishing status window should display a green tick and the message 'Publishing Completed'. The next step is to upload the second page – and its accompanying photograph. Close the Publishing status window and use the tab at the top of the editing window to switch to test2.htm.

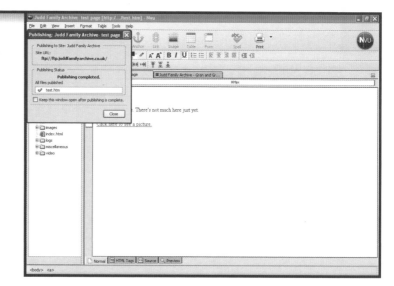

Once again, save the file and then click File > Publish As. This time, we need to make a few changes: tick the box next to 'Include images and other files' and then type 'images' in the 'Use this site subdirectory' field. Click Publish when you've done this.

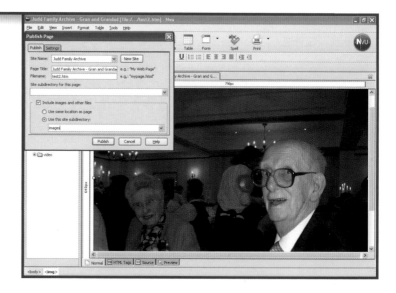

Once again, the Publishing status window will appear, but this time it lists two files instead of one because it's uploading the image as well as the web page. Once you see two green ticks, your test pages have been uploaded to the internet. Close Nvu and open Internet Explorer.

If everything's gone according to plan, your pages should now be on the internet and accessible from anywhere in the world. To find out if they are, reconnect to the internet if you've come offline in the meantime and type **www.juddfamilyarchive.co.uk/test.htm** in your web browser. The first test page should appear. Click the link and you'll see the photo page. Your family tree site will be just as easy to make – and it'll be much, much funkier.

Taking it further

At this juncture, let us remind you that you can add just about anything to your family archive. We'll be looking at scrapbooks later (see p150), where files are tied to individual members of the family tree. However, these files will only be seen by visitors who go to that family member's dedicated web page. You might want to offer some files to all visitors to your site, in which case the best bet is to link to them directly from the home page. For instance, you could have a line that reads: 'To see my interview with Great Auntie Gertrude, click here' – where 'here' is a hyperlink that points to a video clip. We show you how to design your archive home page on p158–163.

PART 6 Genealogy software

PART

We are family

We met Charles John Judd earlier and from this point forth he's going to be our hero. Charles, you see, has been researching his family tree. Indeed, his research is going swimmingly: he can now trace his family back to his great-grandparents on his father's side, and he's made a lot of progress in tracing their other descendants, including details of distant relatives such as great-aunts and great-uncles. There's more than enough information for Charles to start working on his family tree website.

From paper to PC

Charles has already sketched out a basic family tree on paper. It's always a good idea to do this at the outset, as it makes your ancestry easy to understand at a glance and obvious discrepancies or gaps should leap out at you.

But now Charles wants to start entering this information into the computer. For this, he'll use a program called Heritage Family Tree Deluxe (**www.individualsoftware.com**), which costs around £35 from Amazon (**www.amazon.co.uk**).

A glance at the superstore shelves will tell you that genealogy software abounds, and it's perfectly possible that you'll find an alternative program that you prefer to Heritage Family Tree

Heritage Family Tree Deluxe.

Deluxe. However, *all* genealogy software works in pretty much the same way and to much the same end. We – or rather Charles – had to work with something in the workshops ahead, so Heritage Family Tree Deluxe it is for us; if you choose differently, the same principles apply and you should be able to achieve the same overall result.

What we want to do

As you'll see from the next few workshops, using a computer to record your genealogical data is very easy. But it also enables you to do some very clever things. Once the information is stored in the computer, you can view it in a variety of ways, print out various reports and explore the details and relationships of individual ancestors or their descendants. You can also attach all kinds of information to each individual, including notes, details of important events and even multimedia files such as sound clips, video footage or photographs.

One of the things you'll notice in our first workshop is that you don't need to have exhaustive information about every single person in your family tree. In some cases Charles has only been able to discover a few snippets about his ancestors. For example, he knows that a couple were married but doesn't know when they tied the knot, or he knows what year someone was born but doesn't know the exact date, or he knows the name of a distant cousin's mother but not the name of the father. That's fine: Heritage Family Tree Deluxe is quite happy with incomplete information. The further back in time you go the more difficult it can be to get exact dates or detailed information, and as a result the software enables you to enter as much or as little information as you've been able to discover.

Over the next few pages, then, we'll do three things. We'll learn how to use Heritage Family Tree Deluxe for storing the fruits of your research; we'll find out how to view and publish the results of your research; and we'll find out how easy it is to turn everything into a website that your relatives can view from anywhere in the world.

Genealogy software abounds, servicing a tremendous public interest in root-tracing and website-building.

PART  # Get your family tree ready for the web

In this workshop we'll discover how to use Heritage Family Tree Deluxe to create a genealogical database that you can use to organise your research. We'll discover how to enter your own details and those of your immediate ancestors; how to widen the scope to include your extended family; and how to enter incomplete data or store information about relatives who've been married more than once. Once we've done that, we'll quickly turn that information into clickable web pages that you can use to navigate your family history.

When you run Heritage Family Tree Deluxe for the first time, you'll be asked to choose a few quick preferences. These apply to any new project you create. You can change the settings later but for now stick with the default options. Click OK to continue.

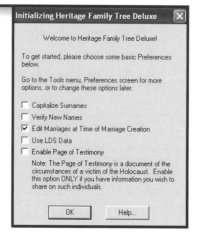

You'll be presented with four options: New, Open, Search and Collaborate. As we don't have any information stored in the program, we need to create a new project where we'll store all the information about the family tree. To do this, click the New button.

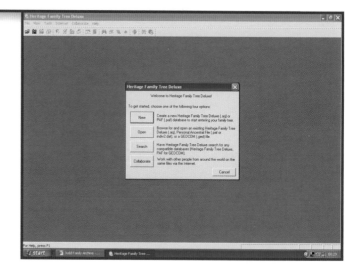

Heritage Family Tree Deluxe will now ask you to choose a name for your project. In this example, we've used 'juddfamily'. By default your project will be stored in your computer's My Documents folder, but you can put it anywhere on your hard disk. Click Create when you've chosen a filename.

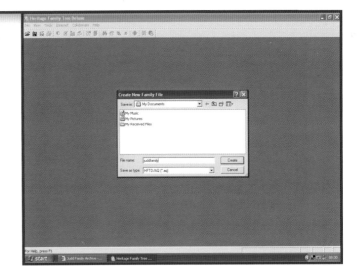

We're nearly ready to start entering information in the program. The Tip of the Day window appears whenever you launch Heritage Family Tree Deluxe and provides some quick tips on using the program; but if you'd rather not see tips when the program runs, uncheck the Show Tips at Startup box. Click Close to continue.

If you're connected to the internet you can check the Heritage Family Tree Deluxe website to see if there any updates available for the software. If you wish, you can tell the program not to remind you for another week or not to remind you ever again.

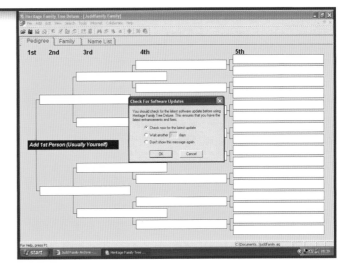

Now that the software has stopped asking questions, it's time to add information about your family to your project. As you can see, the on-screen family tree is blank except for the bit that says 'Add 1st Person (Usually Yourself)'. Click that box to start adding information.

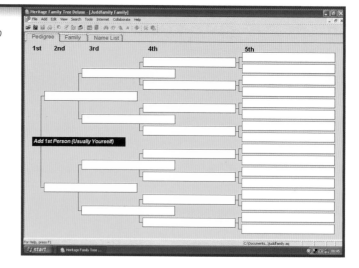

You can now start entering details about yourself into the dialog box. You don't have to fill out all the boxes; just enter whatever information you wish and fill in any gaps later on. Don't worry about all the extra tabs and buttons on this screen either; just concentrate on entering the surname and given names.

Unfortunately, there's a rather annoying bug in Heritage Family Tree Deluxe: even when you've set the program to use British dates, it still expects you to enter details in the American format. That means you'll need to reverse the order of the day and month, so for example the 12th of October would be entered as 10/12 instead of the British 12/10. You'll need to remember this whenever you enter dates into the program.

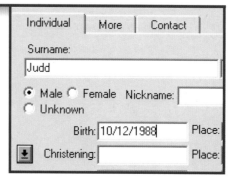

Check that the date appears correctly and then click Save. You'll now be taken to the Family screen, which shows the information you've just added and provides some new boxes. The 'Root Person' is you (or in this example, Charles Judd). The next step is to add details of the parents.

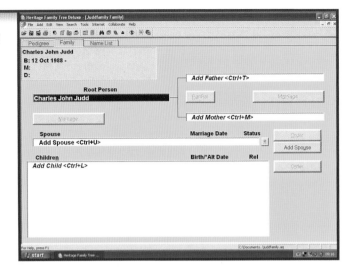

Click the box that says 'Add Father' and you'll see the same dialog box as before. Enter as much information as you can about your father and watch out for that annoying date bug: 3 September 1950 needs to be entered as 9/3/1950. Click Save when you've added the information.

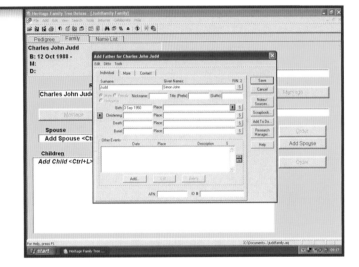

Instead of returning you to the Family screen, the program displays a new dialog box. This enables you to add details of your parents' marriage. We'll enter the date of our father's marriage (again, in US format) but nothing else. Click Save when you've entered the appropriate details.

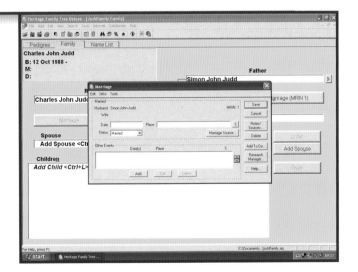

You'll be returned to the Family page and this time the name of your father will appear in the appropriate box. Unsurprisingly enough, the next step is adding details of your mother. To do this, click the Add Mother box and you'll see the familiar dialog box where you can enter her details. Remember to use your mother's maiden name rather than her married name or things could get confusing later!

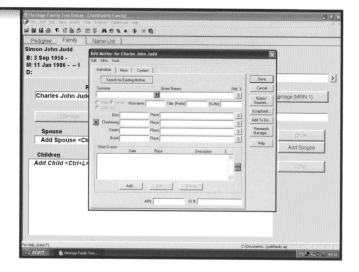

When you entered your details and those of your father, the program asked you to specify each person's sex; that option is greyed out here because the program, naturally enough, assumes that your mother is female. Once again, click Save when you're ready. This time you won't be asked to enter details of your mother's marriage, because the program automatically links her with your father.

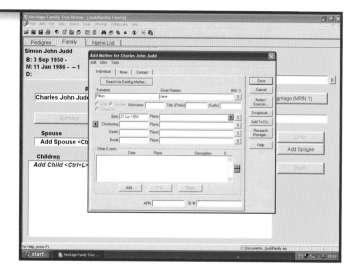

Once again you'll be taken back to the Family page, and as you can see there's the beginning of a family tree on screen. The next person we want to add is a sibling. To do that, we'll need to look at the Family page for your mother. To the right of your mother's name you'll see an arrow; click that to go to her page.

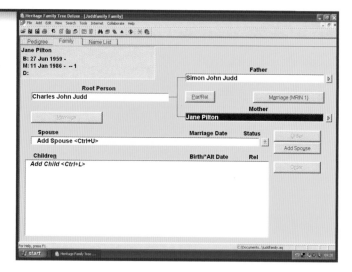

Under your mother's name you'll see your father's name in the Spouse section; below that, there's a box marked Children, in which your name already appears. Click the Add Child text to add details of your brother or sister. Once again, you'll need to enter dates in the US format (we'll stop reminding you about that now).

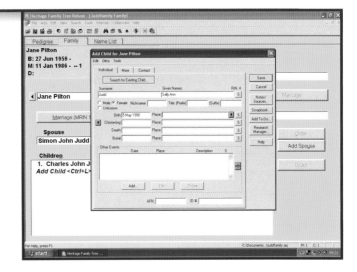

If everything's gone according to plan, you should now see the Family page for your mother. In the Spouse section, you'll see your father's name and the date of their marriage; in the Children section, you should see your name and the names of any siblings.

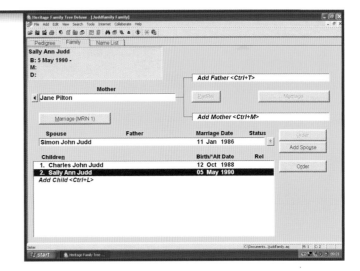

Now we want to add details of your father's parents. To do this we'll need to go to your father's Family page. Double-click his name in the Spouse field or select Search > Relationship Search from the menu bar, then select your father's name, and click OK.

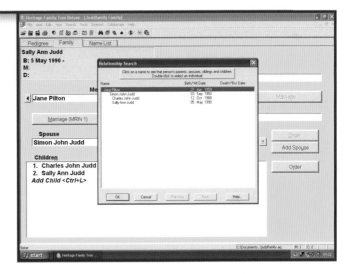

Whichever option you choose, you'll now see the Family page about your dad together with details of his wife and children. The next step is to add details about his father (your paternal grandfather). To do this, click the Add Father box to the right of the screen.

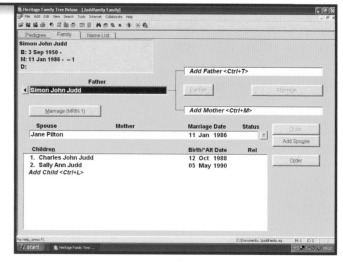

We're back to the familiar data entry screen. As you'd expect, you can now enter the information about your grandfather. In this case, the person has died, so we'll enter the appropriate date in the box marked Death. Click Save when you've entered all the appropriate information.

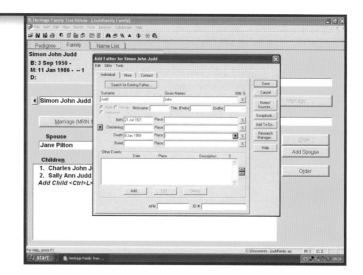

Heritage Family Tree Deluxe will now prompt you for details of your grandfather's marriage. If you don't know the details or don't want to enter them just now, you can click the Cancel button to skip this question. If you do know the details, enter them in the appropriate fields and then click Save.

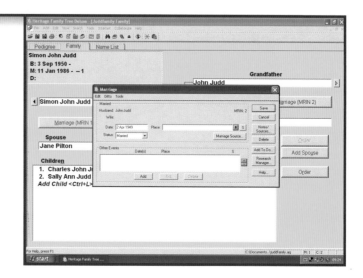

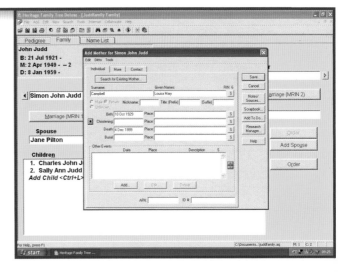

You'll now be taken to the Family page for your father – not your grandfather – and you'll see that the section for his dad's name has been filled in. Now it's time to add the details of your grandmother. Click the Add Mother link at the right of the screen and enter her details in the dialog box.

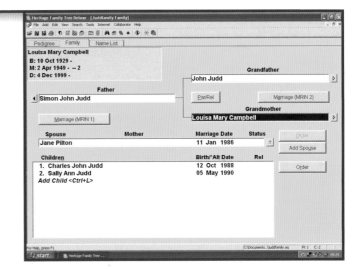

Once again you'll be returned to the Family page about your father. As you can see, things are starting to take shape: the screen now shows the name of your mother, you and your siblings, your grandfather and your grandmother. The labels above each name indicate their relationship to you, so Grandfather means your grandfather.

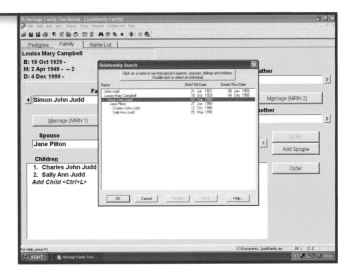

You've now entered enough information to create a basic family tree, and you can explore this in a number of ways. You'll see that many names have arrows next to them. For example, there's an arrow to the left of your father's name; clicking on that arrow moves back one step, which means it'll show the Family page about you. Clicking in the other direction, as you'd expect, moves further up the family tree. You can also find people by selecting Search > Relationship Search from the menu bar.

Another way to view your family tree data is by clicking on the Pedigree tab at the top left-hand corner of the main window. This shows you a bigger view of your family tree, and once again you can use arrows to move around. In this screenshot we're looking at the family tree starting with your father; if you click the arrow at the left, you'll see the family tree starting with you.

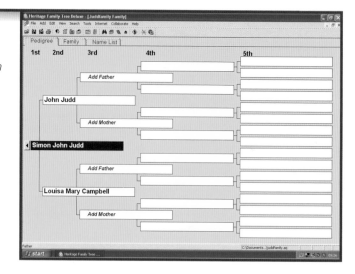

We've already entered details about your paternal grandparents; now it's time to enter information about your great-grandparents. You can do this from the Pedigree window. To the bottom right of your father's name, you'll see your grandmother's name; immediately below and to the right of her name, you'll see the text 'Add Mother'. Click this to enter details of your great-grandmother.

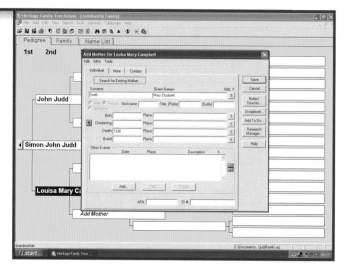

Because we haven't yet entered details of your great-grandfather, Heritage Family Tree Deluxe now asks for details of your great-grandmother's marriage. When you enter details about your great-grandfather, the program will automatically use this information. Click Save to continue.

You'll be returned to the Pedigree page, and the name of your great-grandmother now sits proudly in the family tree. As you'd expect, you can now enter the details of your great-grandfather by clicking on the Add Father box that sits just above your grandmother's name.

Once again it's back to the Pedigree page and, as you can see, the family tree is coming together quite nicely. As before, you can move around the family tree by using the arrows or you can click the Family tab at the top of the screen to see more details about a person.

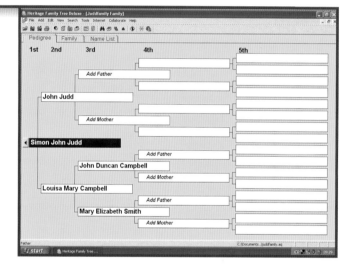

You can now continue to add details of your relatives by going to each person's Family page and then using the appropriate boxes to enter the names of their children, parents or spouses. For example, in this screenshot we're looking at your great-grandfather. You'll see your grandmother's name in the Children section. If – as in this case – your grandmother had a sibling, you'd add their details by clicking the Add Child box.

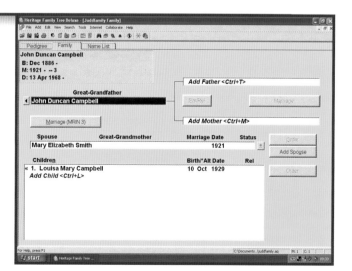

In this example we're looking at Charles Judd's grand-uncle, that is, his grandmother's brother. You'll see that the names of your great-grandparents (your grand-uncle's parents) already appear in the appropriate boxes. If your grand-uncle was married, you'd add details of his wife by clicking on the Add Spouse box. She would be your grand-aunt. Are you keeping up?

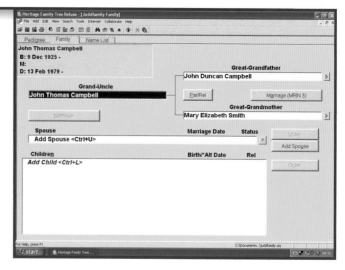

What's interesting about grand-uncles and grand-aunts is that they form a new branch of your family tree. Their children and their children's children will be part of your family tree, but they'll be distant relatives. For example, the child of your grand-uncle and grand-aunt would be your first cousin, um, one time removed.

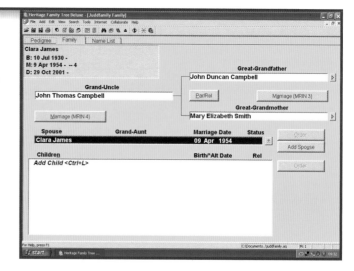

This is where the terms used to describe your relatives can get a little complicated. If your great-aunt and great-uncle's child is your first cousin one time removed, then his spouse would be – take a deep breath – the wife of your first cousin one time removed. Or in this case, the first wife of your first cousin one time removed – Duncan Thomas Campbell was married twice.

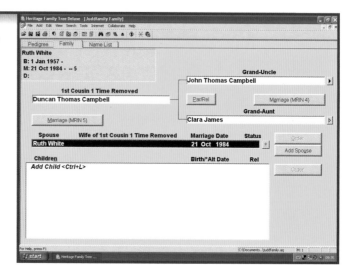

Heritage Family Tree Deluxe wouldn't be much cop if it couldn't cope with multiple marriages, and the good news is that adding a second marriage is simple. Once you've entered the details of a relative's first wife, simply click the Add Spouse button. You can now enter the details of your relative's second wife.

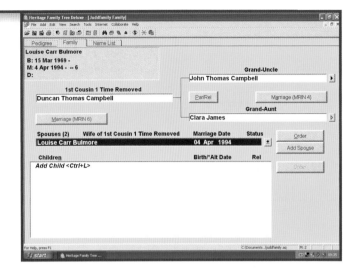

The program can also cater for families where some of the children were from the first marriage, and some of the children were from the second marriage. To enter details of the first wife's children, select her name in the Spouse field and then click Add Child. Enter the child's details in the usual way. When you return to the Family screen, select the second wife's name and repeat the process for her children.

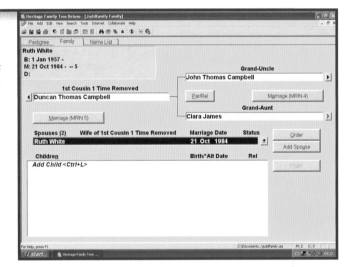

If you ever get lost, you can find people immediately by clicking on the Name List tab at the top of the screen. This displays a list of everybody that you've entered information about, and you can see their details by clicking on their name and then clicking on the Family tab.

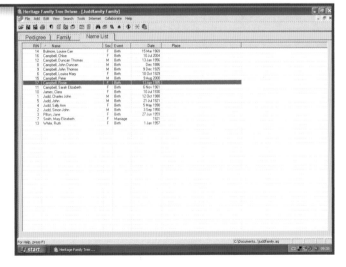

66

We mentioned that the program can cope with details of multiple marriages for the same person; on a related topic, it also enables you to enter details of children born outside of marriage or for whom the full details of their parents aren't available. The Spouse field isn't compulsory, so if someone wasn't married or if you haven't been able to get details of their husband, you can leave it blank.

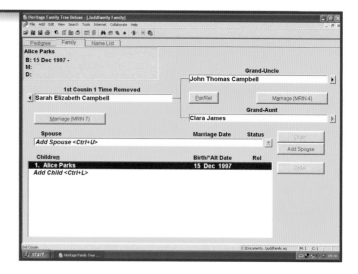

67

You can see where someone appears on the family tree at any time by clicking on the Pedigree tab at the top of the screen. In this example, we're looking at the details of Alice Parks, Charles Judd's second cousin. Charles has been able to trace her details as far back as her maternal great-grandparents, who are also Charles Judd's great-grandparents.

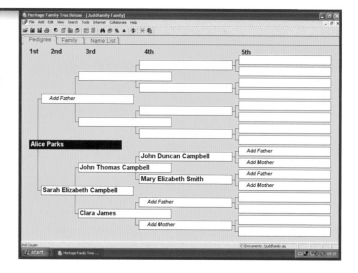

68

This is the same screen but this time we're looking at Charles Judd's position on the family tree. This layout makes it easy to see where there might be some gaps in your research. For example, Charles has been very successful at tracing his father's side of the family, but hasn't been able to trace his mother's family just yet.

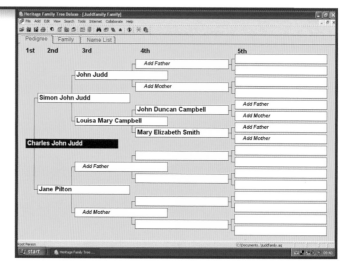

There's now enough information to publish a basic website. To do this, click the Internet menu and then choose *Publish Web Page*. You can ignore most of these options, but make sure that the 'starting person' is you or the website will be incomplete. We'll come back to the other options in a later workshop: for now, click Next.

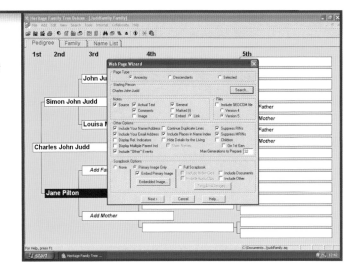

The program will now tell you that 'address information may be incomplete' but don't worry about this. Click Yes, and then Yes again when it asks if you want to continue without an email address. In the next dialog box that appears, give your site a description and add a few words to the 'introduction' field. Click Finish when you've done this.

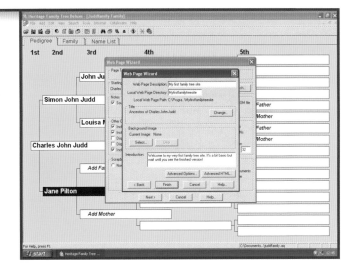

You'll now be asked whether you want to use the 'default background image'. Click Yes and you'll see a message telling you that your site has been created. Click OK to continue. When the program asks if you'd like to view the page in your browser, click Yes; you'll now see your first family tree site. We won't upload it to your web space just yet, though, because we're going to make it look much more impressive first.

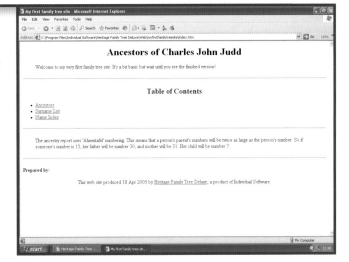

PART  # Different views

In our last workshop we discovered how to enter family tree information into the Heritage Family Tree Deluxe program. Now that we've got the information in our computer, we're going to discover the different ways that we can view and publish the details of our family.

To follow this tutorial, you'll need to install a program called Charting Companion (if you haven't already done so). This program comes free with Heritage Family Tree Deluxe and it's on the same installation CD: just pop the CD into your computer and choose 'Install Charting Companion' from the menu. Alternatively, you can browse the CD from My Computer: look for a folder called CC and run the Setup program you'll find in that folder.

The Charting Companion program produces many of its charts in a file format called PDF, which is short for Portable Document Format. To view these files, you'll need to have a copy of the (free) Adobe Reader program. If it's not already installed on your PC, download the program from **www.adobe.com/products/acrobat/readstep2.html** *and install it.*

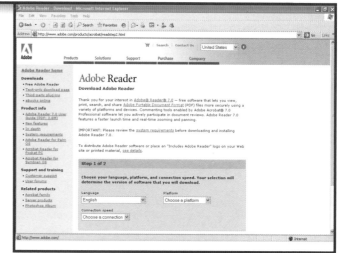

When you run Charting Companion for the first time, it will ask whether you want to search for family database files. Click the Yes button and the program will scour your hard disk for family information. Because it can understand the files created by Heritage Family Tree Deluxe, you won't need to re-enter any details.

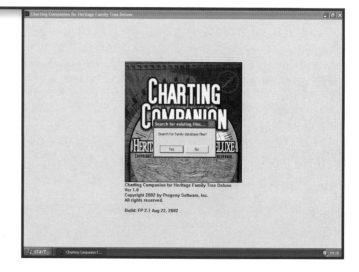

The program will now finish loading and the help file will pop up in the foreground. This gives you an overview of what Charting Companion can do and explains some of the terminology, such as Bow Tie Chart. Once you've had a look, close this window.

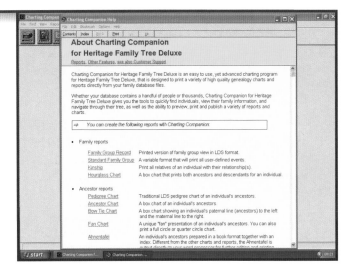

You'll now be given a choice of two files to open: SAMPLEFAMILY.AQ, which is the sample file that Heritage Family Tree Deluxe creates for its tutorials; and the file you created to store your family tree data, which in our case is called JUDDFAMILY.AQ. Click this file and then on the OK button.

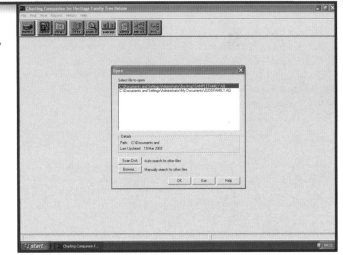

Charting Companion will now show you the information for the 'root person', which will usually be yourself (or in our case, Charles Judd). You can use the arrows at the bottom of the screen to move between individuals' details. When you run a report or chart, Charting Companion will use the currently selected record as the focus. So, for example, if Charles Judd is the current record, any charts we create will be based on Charles's particular branch of the family tree.

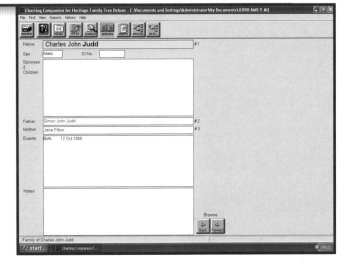

Charting Companion can provide information in two ways: as on-screen views, or as PDF documents that you can save, print, email or stick on the internet. We'll look at the first option first. From the toolbar at the top of the screen, click Views and then select Ancestor View from the dialog box. Click OK to continue.

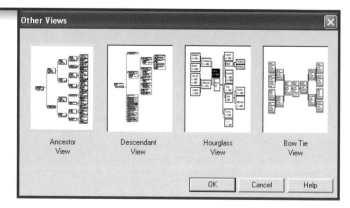

You'll now be presented with a list of options. This tells the program what information to include in a view. For example, you can limit your view to a couple of generations, or include details of siblings. For now we'll stick with the default options. Click the OK button to continue.

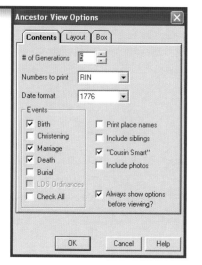

After a few seconds, the screen will display your chosen view: in this case, Charles Judd's ancestors. The view won't show other branches of the family tree, only direct relations. Now for something a bit more ambitious: go back to the toolbar and click the button marked 'Ancestr.'.

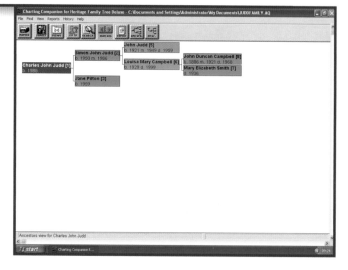

The Ancestor Reports dialog box should now appear on your screen. As you can see, there are five different ancestor reports to choose from. We'll start with the familiar Pedigree report, as this is the simplest option. Make sure that the Pedigree option is selected and then click the OK button.

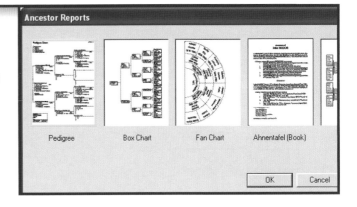

Once again, you'll be presented with a range of options – although they're slightly different from the options we had when we created an ancestor view. Again, you can limit the report to a number of generations, specify whether the report should include record numbers and so on, but we'll stick with the default options. Click Preview to have a look at the report.

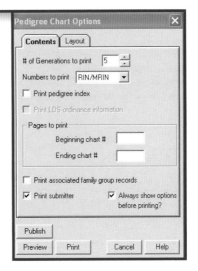

After a few seconds Adobe Reader will open and you'll see your Pedigree chart inside it. You can use the toolbar to zoom in and out, and you can save or print the chart. For now, just close Adobe Reader and return to Charting Companion.

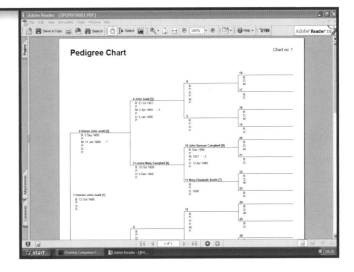

Now for something a bit more visually appealing. Select the
'Ancestr.' button from the toolbar, but this time select the Box
Chart option. This creates a family tree that looks a bit like an
organisation chart, and it's a very effective way to present
genealogical information. Click OK to continue.

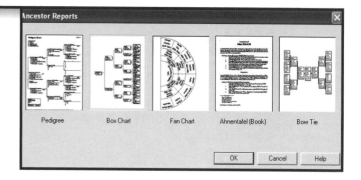

Once again we've got lots of options to choose from: what
information to include, whether to include siblings in the chart,
whether place names should be included and so on. You can
also tweak the chart's layout by using the Layout and Box tabs
at the top of the dialog box. We'll stick with the default options
for now. Click Preview to continue.

Once again Adobe Reader will open and display the results of
your chart. As you can see it's nice and neat, and of course you
can go back to Charting Companion and tweak the layout until
it's perfect. Because this is a PDF document, it opens some
interesting possibilities: you could email this chart or publish it to
your website. We'll discover how to do that in the next workshop.

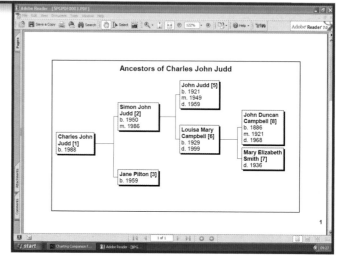

We're pleased with the way this chart looks, so we're going to save it for future reference. In the Adobe Reader program, click the 'Save a Copy' button at the top left of the screen. You may be presented with the warning message shown in our screenshot, but don't worry about it: just click Do Not Show This Message Again and then click on OK.

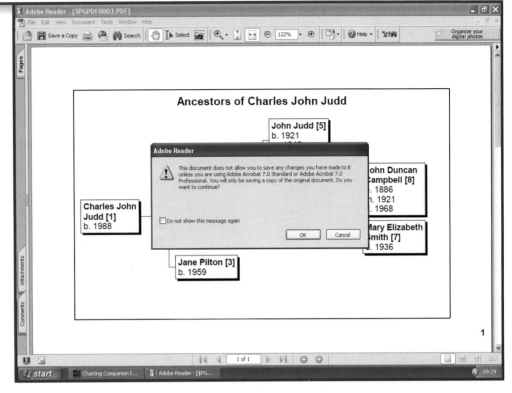

The familiar Save dialog box will now appear. Give your chart a sensible name so you'll be able to find it in future, and store it in a folder such as My Documents (the default option). Once you've done this, go back to Charting Companion and try experimenting with the other chart types and their options. You'll find that it's a lot of fun.

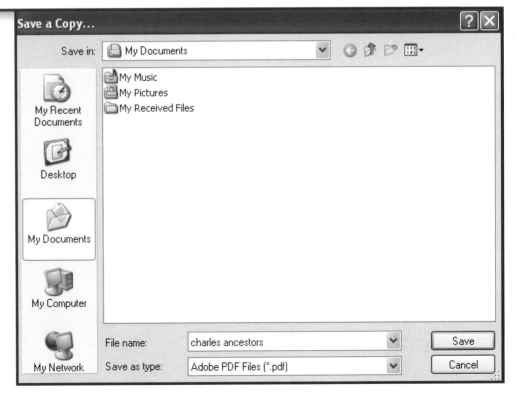

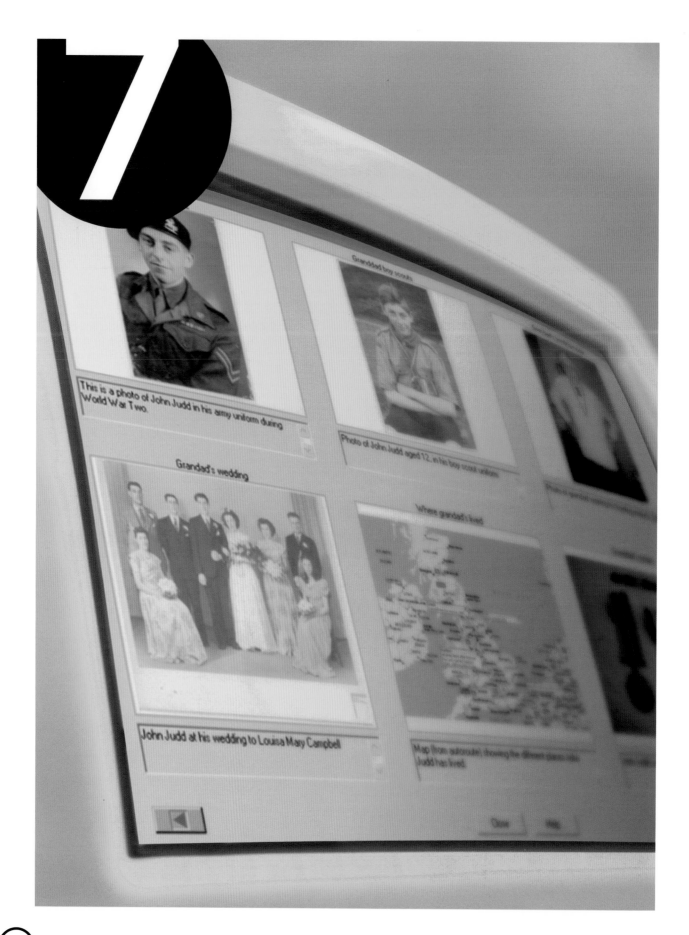

This is a photo of John Judd in his army uniform during World War Two.

Grandad boy scouts

Photo of John Judd aged 12, in his boy scout uniform.

Grandad's wedding

John Judd at his wedding to Louisa Mary Campbell

Where grandad's lived

Map (from autoroute) showing the different places John Judd has lived.

PART **7**

Completing your family archive project

PART  Putting photos on the web

It's time to see the results of all your hard work. We're going to build a smart website that shows off the results of all your research. In the last few workshops, we've explored Heritage Family Tree Deluxe, entered details of family members and discovered how easy it is to create a web page; in this tutorial, we'll combine these different elements to create an online family tree and photo gallery. At the end of this workshop you'll have a living, breathing website where people can explore the family tree and browse through photographs of family members – and as with all the workshops so far, you'll be amazed at how easy it is to do.

In this workshop, we'll do three things. We'll add images to our family tree database; we'll publish our family tree data as a collection of images and web pages; and we'll create a front page for our site that links to the actual family tree. Once we've done those three things, actually putting the site on the internet is as easy as copying files from one folder to another. Don't let the size of this workshop put you off: the whole process doesn't take long and doesn't involve anything scary.

For this workshop, we need to collate the photographs of various family members that we intend to use in our website. Our screenshot shows a fairly typical collection of such images, with typically brief filenames. With a large family tree, it's a very good idea to make your file names as descriptive as possible.

Right-click each filename and select Rename. Instead of names such as 'judd1', 'judd2' and so on, use names that make it crystal-clear what each picture is – 'charlesjohnjuddpic', 'grandadbowling', 'grandadmap', and so on. You'll thank yourself for this later on. Don't use spaces in your file names.

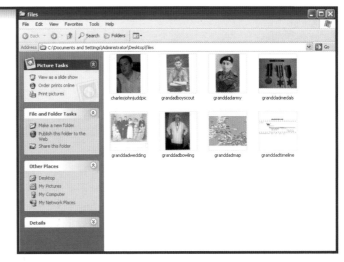

It's a very good idea to store your files in a place where you can find them easily. In this example, we'll put all of our images in the Images folder of our My website folder. When we use these images in our family tree, Heritage Family Tree Deluxe will create a copy of each photo for uploading to the internet.

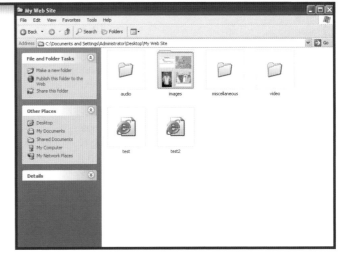

Launch Heritage Family Tree Deluxe. Here we have Charles Judd's family tree once again. We're interested in his grandfather, so double-click John Judd to select him, then double-click his name again to open the Edit window.

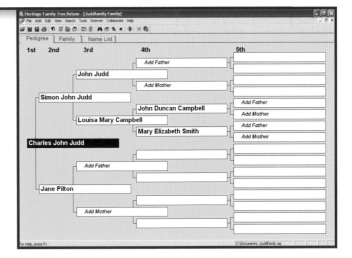

You should now see the familiar Edit Individual window, which we've used again and again to enter details of our family members. This time, though, we need to use a different bit of the Edit window: the Scrapbook. Click the Scrapbook button at the right of the window.

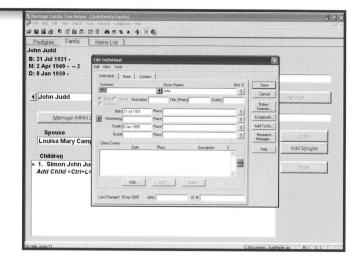

The Scrapbook is where you add photographs and other files associated with a particular family member. To begin with, we'll add the main photo of John Judd. This will appear on his web page. To do this, click the Add...button.

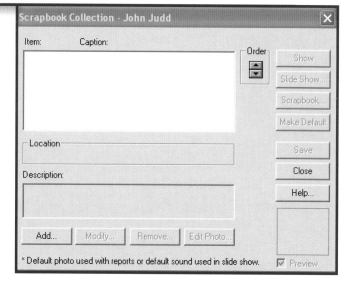

You'll now see the Add Scrapbook Item dialog box. It's blank with one exception. By default, the Item Type is set to 'photo'. If you were adding a video, you'd change this setting. However, we'll stick with images for now, so leave Item Type as it is and click the Browse button.

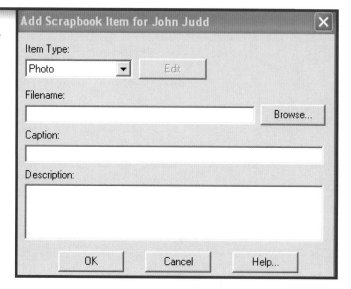

Navigate to the folder where you stored your pictures – in this example, My website\images – and choose the photo you want to use. If you're not sure, tick the Preview box. This displays a little version of each photo so you can be sure you're choosing the right one. Once you've found the image you want, click Open.

You'll be returned to the Add Scrapbook Item dialog box, and this time you'll see that the Filename box has been filled in. Give the photograph a short title in the Caption box and then enter some descriptive text in the Description box. This text will appear on that family member's scrapbook page.

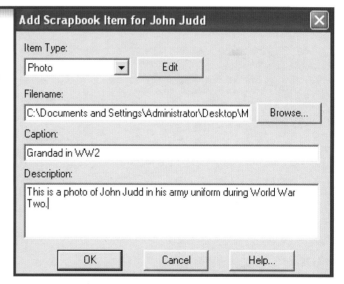

The Scrapbook Collection window will now be displayed, and it should contain the photo you've just added. You'll see an asterisk (*) next to that photo: this means it's the default image, which will appear on John Judd's main web page. Other pictures will only appear in his Scrapbook page.

Using the Add...button, repeat the process for the other images of John Judd. When you've done this, the Scrapbook Collection screen should look like this. You can double-check that you haven't made any typing mistakes by clicking on each photo and reading its description.

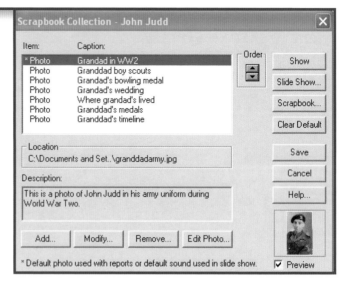

Let's have a look at the Scrapbook for John Judd. To do this, just click the Scrapbook button at the right of the dialog box; after a few seconds, you should see all your images, captions and descriptions. Click Close when you're finished and then click Save.

As you'd expect, you can add items to other family members' scrapbooks by locating their records, double-clicking their name to bring up the Edit Individual window and then clicking on the Scrapbook button. In this screenshot, we're adding an image of Charles John Judd.

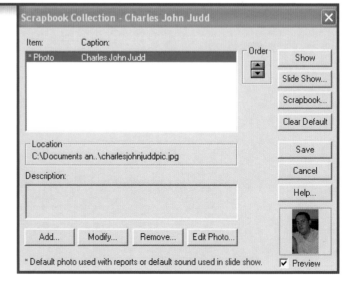

Return to the page for Charles John Judd and click Internet > Create Web Page. You can leave the various options as they are, with two exceptions: the Page Type must be set to 'Ancestry' and the Scrapbook Options should be set to 'Full Scrapbook'. Click Next to continue.

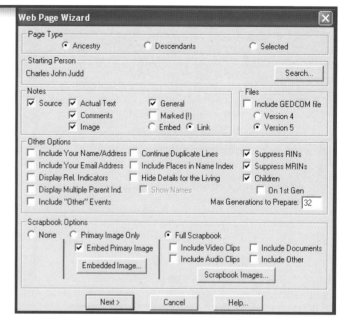

The program will now ask you to give your web page a description, and it will use this description (without spaces) as the name of the folder in which it will store all the site files. If you wish, you can also add some text in the Introduction box.

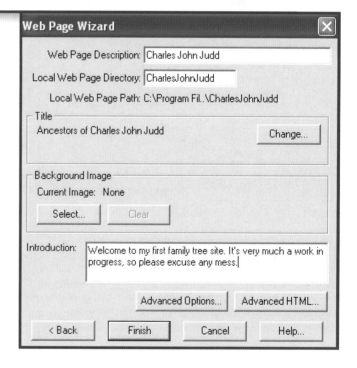

Click the Advanced Options button and you'll see this dialog box. The '3 char. File prefix' will be added to every web page created by Heritage Family Tree Deluxe, and you can change it if you wish; the important bit though, is to uncheck the 'Use Index.htm' button. The index page is always the first page you see in a website and we want to create our own (see Step 26 onwards). Click OK to build the site.

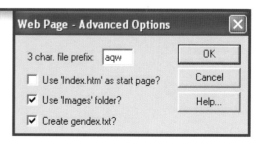

Once Heritage Family Tree Deluxe has created the web pages, it will ask you if you want to view them in your web browser. Answer Yes and you'll see this page, which is the first page of the site. To navigate around the family tree, click the Ancestors link.

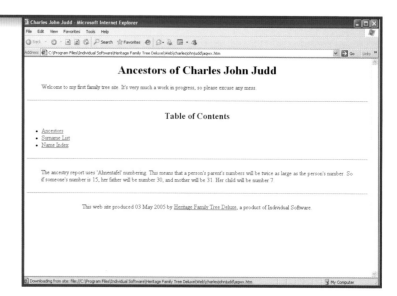

The first bit of information we see is about Charles John Judd himself. Heritage Family Tree Deluxe has automatically included his photograph in the page. You'll see two links on the page: scrapbook takes you to Charles's scrapbook, while Parents continues to explore the family tree. Click Parents to continue.

This page tells us all about Charles's parents. Because we haven't added any images the page is photo-free; it doesn't include a scrapbook link either. However, we're interested in Charles's grandparents, and to find out about them we need to click the Parents link.

Now, you should see the page about Charles's grandparents, John Judd and Louisa Mary Campbell. Once again Heritage Family Tree Deluxe has automatically added a small picture of John Judd; as we haven't yet added a picture of Louisa Campbell, we just see her name instead of her name and picture.

If you click the scrapbook link, you'll be taken to this page – the scrapbook page for Charles Judd's grandfather. As you can see, it displays a small version of each photograph in the scrapbook, and it also includes the titles and descriptions we entered earlier.

The blue borders around each photograph indicate that you can click them; if you do, you'll see a full-size version of the image you've clicked on. As we've seen, the site works perfectly on your computer; now, we need to make it work perfectly on the internet.

We need to move the website files to our website folder.
To do this, you need to open two My Computer windows:
one for your My website folder and one for the Heritage
Family Tree Deluxe files. You'll find the files in
C:\Program Files\Individual Software\Heritage Family Tree
Deluxe\Web\sitename.

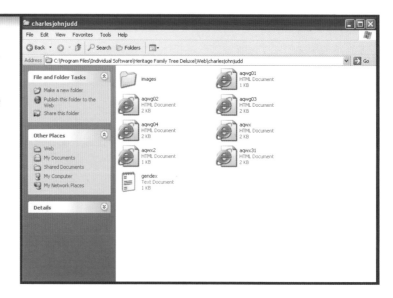

Click the folder containing Heritage Family Tree Deluxe's
website files, select Edit > Select All from the menu,
and drag them over your My website folder. Windows will
ask if you're sure about this; click Yes To All. The files
will now be copied into the My website folder, ready for
us to upload them to the internet.

Once the copying has finished, your My website folder
should look something like this. The files beginning
'aqw' are the actual web pages created by Heritage
Family Tree Deluxe, and you can view them in Internet
Explorer by double-clicking on them. The first such page
is called 'aqwx'.

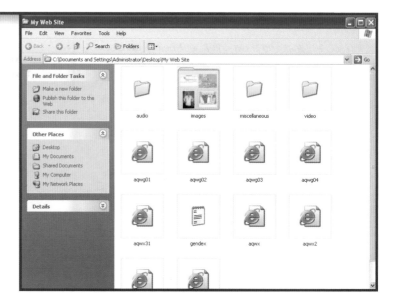

Our site isn't quite ready to go on the internet, but there's very little left to do: we need to create a front page – the index page – for the site, and that's about it. To do this, launch the Nvu web editing program we explored in previous workshops. We'll use this program to create our site's front page.

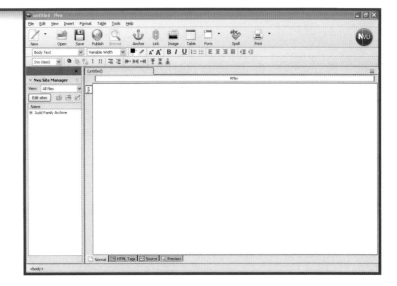

This will be the front page of the entire website, so it's a good idea to have a headline, some introductory text and, finally, a link to the rest of the site. You can put any text you like in here, but make sure you finish with something along the lines of 'Click here to start exploring'.

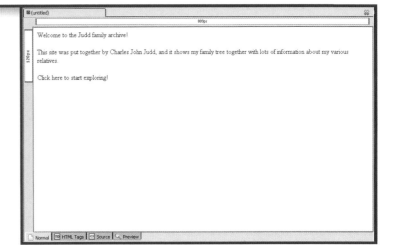

The next step is to add a hyperlink, but before we can do that we need to save the file. Click File > Save, and you'll see the Page Title dialog box as in our screenshot. Give your page a meaningful title, as this is what will appear in visitors' web browsers and search engine results.

Make sure you save your file in the same folder that you're using for your website (in this case, My website) and use the filename 'index'. This is going to be the front page of the entire site. Nvu will automatically add the '.html' suffix when you save the file.

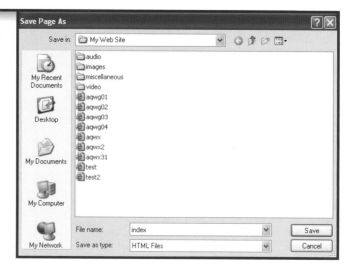

In the editing window, highlight the text that says 'Click here to...' and click the big Link button in the toolbar. You'll now see the Link Properties dialog box. We want to link the front page to the family tree. To do this, click the Choose File button.

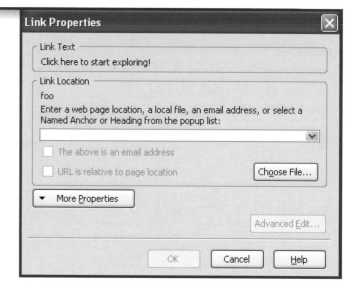

Browse to the My website folder and select the file called 'aqwx' – this is the first web page generated by Heritage Family Tree Deluxe. Once you've done this, close the dialog box and your screen should look something like this, with the link shown in blue text. Save the file and close Nvu.

In Internet Explorer, enter the address
ftp://ftp.juddfamilyarchive.co.uk *(where 'juddfamilyarchive' is
your own domain name). Windows should have remembered
your username and password from the first FTP software
workshop. Resize the window so it only takes up half the screen.*

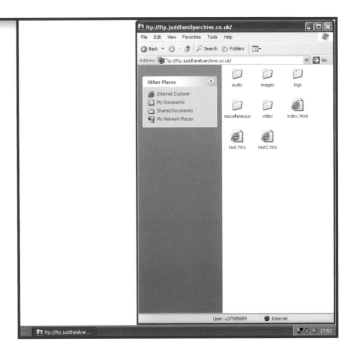

Go to My Computer and navigate to your My website folder, and
then resize the window so it sits next to the FTP folder you
opened in the last step. Go to Edit > Select All, and then drag
all of your files from My website to the FTP folder. The copying
process may take a few minutes.

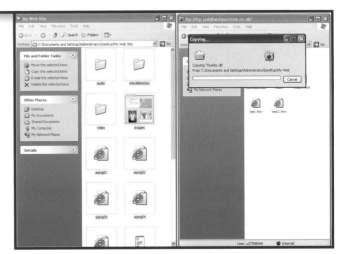

When the copying is finished, close both windows and then open
Internet Explorer. In the address bar, enter
www.juddfamilyarchive.co.uk *(replace 'juddfamilyarchive' with
your own domain name) and the site should appear. You can
now navigate around your family tree – but this time, you're
doing it on the internet and anyone in the world can now do the
same.*

PART  A multimedia scrapbook

As you've already discovered, it's very easy to add photographs to your website – but what if you also want to add video clips, sound clips and document files? You'll be pleased to know that it's just as simple to add these kinds of files to your site. In fact, it's exactly the same process you use for adding photographs.

A word on file formats

Before you think about using multimedia – sound and video – files on the internet, it's very important to consider the file format you need to use. We'd recommend MP3 for sound files – they're reasonably small and work on every kind of computer – and Windows Media for video. The tools you need to create Windows Media clips are free (Windows Movie Maker is included with Windows XP) and the resulting content works on Windows and Apple machines alike. For documents you can add almost any kind of file, but we'd recommend plain text files or Adobe PDF files for maximum compatibility. As with MP3, these files can be read on any computer.

See Appendices 1 and 2 for more on this.

Collate the files you want to use and put them in sensible places, such as your My website > Audio folder for sound clips and My website > Video for video clips. When you've done this, open Heritage Family Tree Deluxe and find the entry for John Judd; then bring up the Edit Individual dialog, click Scrapbook, and click Add.

Select Video Clip as the item type and use the Browse button to locate your video file. Make sure you change the Files of Type dropdown to 'all files': if you don't, you won't see any Windows Media files. Click your video clip and then click on the Open button to select it.

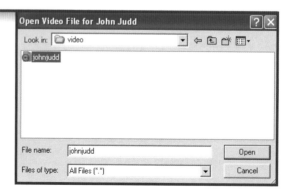

Now add a caption – a short title for your video clip – and then add a more detailed description in the Description field. This information will appear on your finished website so make it as clear as possible; you don't want to confuse your visitors.

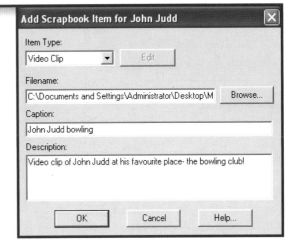

Click OK and you should be returned to the Scrapbook dialog box. If everything's gone according to plan, you should now see your video clip listed underneath the photographs you added in previous workshops. However, as this is a video file rather than a photo you won't see anything in the Preview box in the corner.

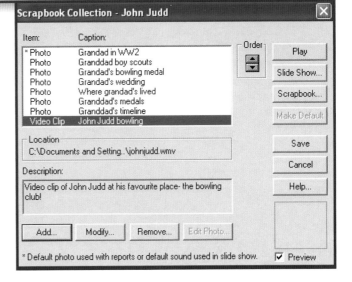

Now repeat the process, but this time click Add and then choose Audio as the kind of file you want to add. Click the Browse button and locate the folder you stored your MP3 file in. In the File Type dropdown at the bottom of this dialog, choose MPEG3 so you can actually see your MP3 files. Select the file you want to use and then click Open.

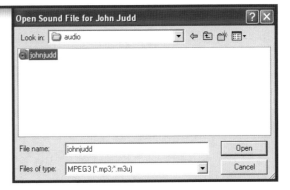

As with your video clip, you need to add some descriptive information so that your visitors will be able to see immediately what the sound clip is for. Give the clip a short title in the Caption field and then add a slightly more detailed explanation in the Description field. Click OK when you've done this.

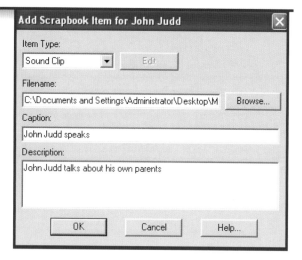

Repeat the process again, but this time tell Heritage Family Tree that you want to include a document. Use the browse button to find the PDF files you created earlier using the Charting Companion. Select the one you want to use and click Open to add it to your scrapbook.

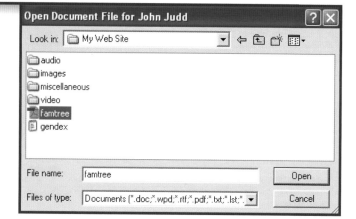

Once again, it's time to add a bit more explanation: the Caption is the title that will appear on the web page next to the document link, while the description appears underneath the caption. Once you've entered these details, click OK to return to the main scrapbook dialog box.

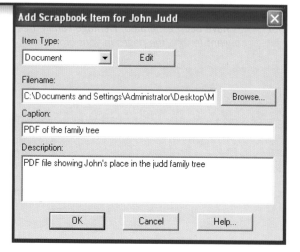

The Scrapbook Collection for John Judd should now list all the photos you added earlier, plus the video clip, the audio clip and the PDF file you've just added. If you'd like to check that the files work OK, select the file you want to check and then click the Show button to launch that file. For example, if you select the PDF and click Show, it will open in the Adobe Reader program.

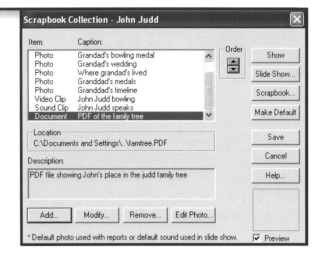

Save your changes and return to the Pedigree page for John Judd. To see if our additions have worked, click Internet > Create Web Page in the menu bar. When the dialog box appears, make sure you tick the boxes at the bottom right of the screen marked 'include video clips', 'include audio clips' and 'include documents'. Click Next to continue and then Finish to create the web pages.

When the web pages have been generated, Heritage Family Tree Deluxe will ask if you want to view the pages in your browser. Choose yes and navigate to John Judd's ancestors page. Here you'll see the link to his scrapbook. Click that link and scroll down to the bottom: you should now see links to your video, audio and PDF files. If you click them, the appropriate files should load. Voila! As in Steps 23–25 on p146, copy these finished pages to your My website folder.

PART **Expanding the database**

There's no such thing as a static family. New additions come along all the time and even ancient relatives require occasional updating. The harder you look for information, the more you will uncover. What you need, then, is an approach that lets you continually modify your records. This is where genealogy software – as opposed to pen and paper – really comes into its own.

Charles Judd's initial research was impressive, but it was also rather one-sided; while he amassed lots of information about his father's side of the family, the information about his maternal ancestors was largely non-existent. However, Charles hasn't stopped researching and he's now managed to amass lots of information about his relatives on his mother's side of the family. In this workshop, we'll discover how that information can be added to the existing database.

In Heritage Family Tree Deluxe, open your database if it isn't already open. We're working with the Judd family again. As you can see, Charles's family tree is somewhat lop-sided; but now that he's compiled some further research, he can make the tree more balanced.

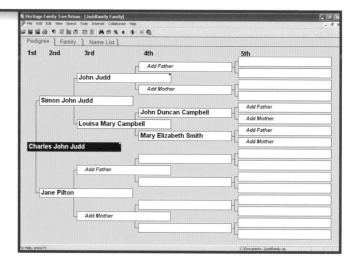

Click Charles's mother, Jane Pilton, and then click on the Add Mother link below and to the right of her name. You can now enter details of Jane's mother. Remember to watch out for the American date formats, so in this example you would enter 16th October 1937 as 10/16/1937.

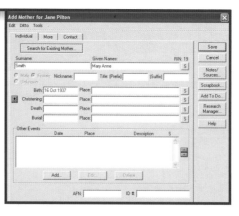

Click Save and the program will now ask for details of Mary Anne Smith's marriage. Enter the date – once again using American date formats – and then click the Save button to return to the family tree view. You won't be asked for details of Mary Anne's husband just yet.

4

Now it's time to add the details of Jane Pilton's father. As you'd expect, you do this by clicking on the Add Father box above and to the right of Jane Pilton's name; this will open the Edit Individual dialog box, where you can enter the necessary information.

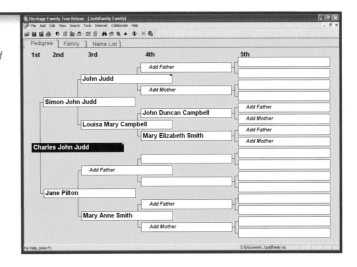

5

Our information on John James Pilton is rather sketchy, but don't worry: Heritage Family Tree Deluxe is quite happy with even the most basic information about people. Once you've entered the details of John James Pilton, click Save to update your database and return to the family tree.

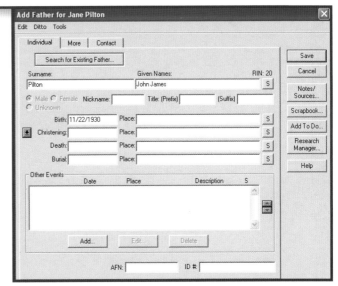

6

You can now enter details of the rest of your maternal ancestors in exactly the same way: the Add Father and Add Mother boxes to the right of each person's name will take you to the Edit Individual page, where you can add as much or as little information as you have.

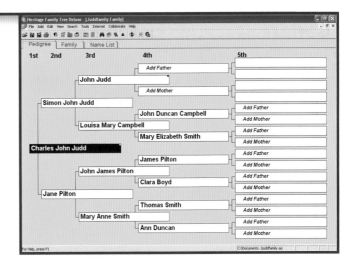

Of course, in most cases your maternal ancestors will have had
several children. For example, Thomas Smith and Ann Duncan
didn't just have Charles's grandmother (Mary Ann), but another
child too. Although the child isn't a direct ancestor of Charles,
he's still part of the extended family tree. To add his details, click
Thomas Smith's name and then on the Family tab. Use the Add
Child link to add the relevant information.

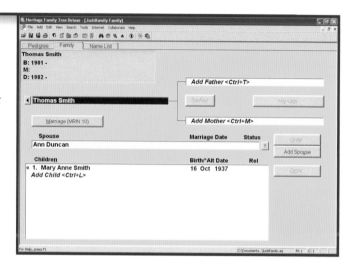

It's always a good idea to return to the very beginning of the
family tree whenever you've finished adding new information;
otherwise you can often get lost in the various branches! To do
this at any time, click the Name List tab at the top of the
screen, click the name you want to view – in this case, Charles
John Judd – and then on the Pedigree tab to see the family tree.

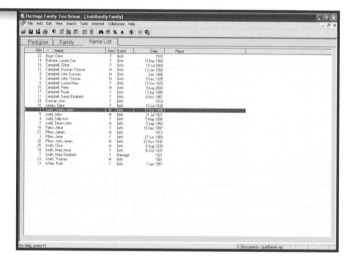

Charles's mother also had a sister, Ann. To add her to the family
tree, we need to click Charles's maternal grandmother, Mary
Ann Smith, and then on the Family tab to see details of her
family. You'll see that Jane Pilton is already in the Children list;
use Add Child to enter details of Jane's sister.

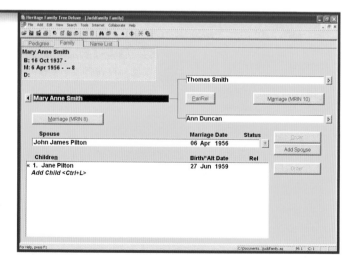

Jane's sister was married, and we can add the details of her husband in the Family view by clicking on the white box that says Add Spouse. This brings up the Edit Individual dialog box, which you can use to enter the details of Charles's maternal uncle.

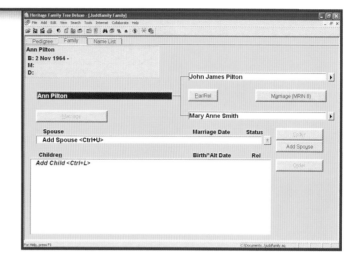

Ann and William Pilton have a child, Charles's cousin Daniel. To add his details we stay with the Family tab, but this time we use the Add Child link to add details of Daniel. When you've done this, click the Name List tab at the top of the screen and then on Charles Judd's name.

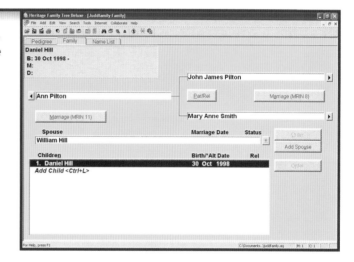

Click the Pedigree tab and you should see a family tree such as the one in our screenshot. It's much more balanced than before because our database now contains details of Charles's maternal and paternal ancestors. The information is nearly ready to publish online, but before we do that we've got one more workshop.

PART 7

Designing your archive home page

Charles has tracked down even his most elusive ancestors, amassed audio clips, purloined pictures and stuffed his software with a feast of family information, so all that's left is to publish it – right? Well, yes and no. While all the information we need to put on the internet is indeed in our database, the finished web pages aren't as good-looking as they could be. As you'll discover in this workshop, that's very easy to change.

Over the next few pages we'll publish our complete family tree as a website. We'll use the free Nvu web design program (which we explored in earlier workshops) to create an attractive front page, or home page. We'll introduce you to some design tricks of the trade and turn a fairly flat home page into something much more interesting.

It's worth noting that you can publish directly from within Heritage Family Tree Deluxe and most other genealogy software programs. However, because we've chosen to use Nvu to design the archive front page, we want to take the web pages that Heritage Family Tree Deluxe creates, link them to this page and then upload them separately.

We also point out again that you can link to any files you like directly from the front page. For instance, Charles might want to include hyperlinks to a PDF of his personal Bow Tie Chart (see p131) or a page of personal photos. He might also include a hyperlink to the home page of his personal Google Group so that other members of the family can chip in with their comments and knowledge (see p47). With hyperlinks on his home page, the scope is endless.

As with our previous tutorials, don't let the number of steps put you off: we've crossed every T and dotted every i to make sure that the whole process is crystal clear. Nothing in this tutorial is difficult or requires a lot of effort; and, as you'll discover, a few little tweaks can make a big difference.

If Heritage Family Tree Deluxe isn't already loaded, launch the program and then click the Pedigree tab. Navigate to the first person in the family tree, Charles John Judd, and make sure that his name is highlighted: if it isn't, then the website won't start with his details.

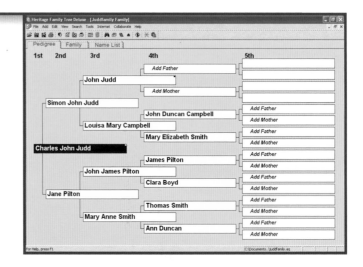

Click Internet > Create Web Page and set the options you want to use in your website. If you've added sound, video or documents to the scrapbook for any individuals then make sure the Full Scrapbook, Include Video Clips, Include Audio Clips and Include Documents boxes are checked.

Click the Next button and give your page a description; this will appear in visitors' web browsers and in search engine results. Heritage Family Tree Deluxe will automatically complete the 'Local Web Page Directory' field; take a note of this as you'll need to find this folder in a moment. When you've done that, click the Advanced Options button.

You can leave most of the settings unchanged, but make sure the 'Use Index.html as start page' box is NOT checked. When you've done this, click OK and then get Heritage Family Tree Deluxe to create your web pages. Close the program when the process is complete.

On your desktop, double-click My Computer and navigate to C:\Program Files\Individual Software\Heritage Family Tree Deluxe\Web. You took a note of a folder name in Step 3; this is the folder you want to open now. In our example it's the TheJuddFamilyArchive folder.

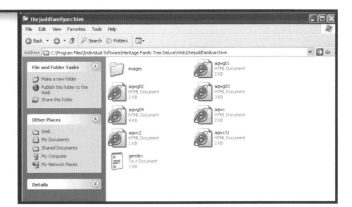

Leaving the TheJuddFamilyArchive folder open, double-click your My website folder to open it as well. Now return to the TheJuddFamilyArchive folder, select everything, and drag the files over to the My website folder. When Windows asks if you'd like to replace the existing files or folders, click Yes To All. This procedure copies the web pages created by Heritage Family Tree Deluxe into your web folder.

It's time to do some tweaking. Close both of the My Computer windows and launch the Nvu web editing program; once you've done this, click the Open button and select the file index.htm from your My website folder. You should see a page like the one in our screenshot. Do you remember that back in Step 31 on p148, we hyperlinked 'Click here to start exploring' to a file named aqwx? This is always the opening page in a heritage Family Tree Deluxe project. Because we have just copied the program's web pages to our local Web site folder, this hyperlink will now launch Charles's family tree.

Place the cursor immediately before the word 'Welcome' and press Enter a few times; this will move the text slightly down the page. Now click the Table button. You should see the dialogue box in our screenshot, and it should show a 2x2 table. Click OK to continue.

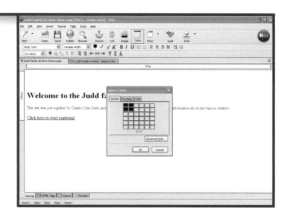

Your page should look like this, with a 2x2 box sitting above the text (each section of the table is called a 'cell'). We're going to use this table to improve our page's layout. While it looks a bit complicated it's actually very, very easy. Our table won't even appear in the finished version – it'll be an invisible helper.

Highlight the table and click Table > Table Properties. This enables you to tweak the table's settings; click Table Alignment, change it to Centre, and click OK. We'll now make the table a bit thinner; to do this, grab the left hand 'wall' of the table and drag it to the right with your mouse. When you let go, the table should have shrunk in size.

Your page should now look something like this, with the table sitting in the top middle of the screen. It can be a bit fiddly, so don't worry if it takes a few attempts before you successfully resize it.

Welcome to the Judd family archive!

This site was put together by Charles John Judd, and it shows my family tree together with lots of information about my various relatives.

Click here to start exploring!

Now to add some text. Highlight the 'Welcome to the Judd Family Archive' text and then click it with the mouse – but don't let go of the mouse button. Instead, drag the text over the top left-hand cell in the table, and then let go of the mouse. The headline should now appear in the table.

Welcome to the Judd family archive!

This site was put together by Charles John Judd, and it shows my family tree together with lots of information about my various relatives.

Click here to start exploring!

We only need one table cell for our headline, so we'll get rid of the extra cell at the right. To do this, use the mouse to highlight the top two cells of the table; if you right-click, you'll see a menu of table options. Click Join Selected Cells.

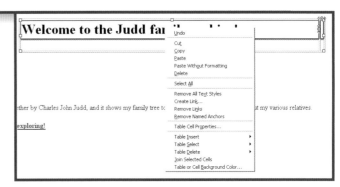

Welcome to the Judd fa...

Undo
Cut
Copy
Paste
Paste Without Formatting
Delete
Select All
Remove All Text Styles
Create Link...
Remove Links
Remove Named Anchors
Table Cell Properties...
Table Insert
Table Select
Table Delete
Join Selected Cells
Table or Cell Background Color...

...ther by Charles John Judd, and it shows my family tree to... ...t my various relatives.

...exploring!

As you can see, our four-cell table has become a three-cell table: there's one big wide cell at the top, and then two smaller cells below it. Let's move the rest of our text, but this time we'll put it in the bottom right cell. To do this, highlight the text, click the Cut icon in the toolbar, click in the bottom right cell and then click the Paste icon.

Welcome to the Judd family archive!

This site was put together by Charles John Judd, and it shows my family tree together with lots of information about my various relatives.

Click here to start exploring!

The text has appeared in the right place but Nvu has made the bottom left-hand cell very small. Don't worry about this, because when we put a photo in there – which we'll do in the very next step – the cell will automatically expand to fit the photo.

Welcome to the Judd family archive!

This site was put together by Charles John Judd, and it shows my family tree together with lots of information about my various relatives.

Click here to start exploring!

Place the cursor in the bottom left-hand cell of the table and then click the Image icon. Navigate to your images folder and choose an appropriate photo; remember to enter Alternate Text too, as not all internet users can see images. You can change your photo's size here too; to do that, click the Dimensions tab.

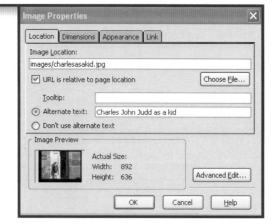

Our photo's a bit big, so we'll make it 300 pixels wide; that's a good size for on-screen viewing. If you click the Constrain box when you resize an image, Nvu will automatically calculate the appropriate size. In this example, it's worked out that if our image is 300 pixels wide, it needs to be 214 pixels high. Hurrah for technology!

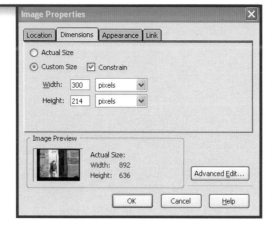

Click OK and then close the Image dialog box. As you'll see from our screenshot, Nvu hasn't just added the image to the appropriate table cell; it's also resized the cell so that it's the perfect size. However, it's all looking a bit cramped so we'll space things out a bit.

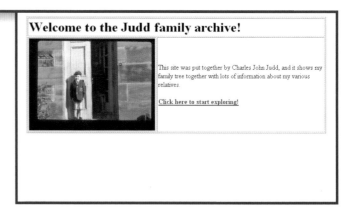

Highlight the table and then click Table > Table Properties. In the section Borders and Spacing, change Border to zero, Spacing to zero and Padding to 20. That means the border of each cell will be invisible, there'll be no space between the table cells, and there'll be a gap of 20 pixels between the border of any cell and the text or photos it contains. It's much easier to see than to read about, so...

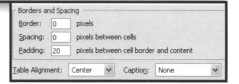

...here's what those changes actually look like. Nvu now shows the cell borders in red; that means the borders will be invisible when you actually publish your web page. Your design is almost complete, so try adding some more text and changing the appearance further by changing the fonts in your page.

Welcome to the Judd family archive!

This site was put together by Charles John Judd, and it shows my family tree together with lots of information about my various relatives.

Click here to start exploring!

It's looking good, isn't it? There's only one more change before we can publish the site: we need to add an email link so visitors can get in touch. Highlight the appropriate text – in our example, 'please email me' – and then click the Link button in the main toolbar.

Enter the appropriate email address in the blank space and then make sure that you tick the 'the above is an email address' button; if the button isn't ticked then the email address won't work. Now, visitors to the site will be able to click this link to send emails to you.

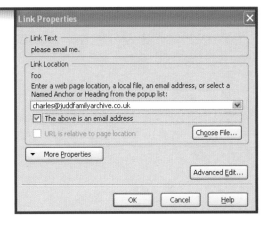

Click OK and then click the Preview tab at the bottom left of the editing window; this shows you exactly how your page will appear on the web. It's a vast improvement on before! Feel free to keep on tweaking; and when you're happy with the results, simply upload your site again by following the steps on p109–111.

PART 8 Introducing GEDCOM

More than just a file format

Although it's quite possible to navigate through the various genealogy websites and do some cutting and pasting, it's also possible to add lots of data to your project very quickly using a technology called GEDCOM.

Joined-up genealogy

GEDCOM stands for Genealogical Data COMmunications and is a standard data format developed by the LDS Church. In much the same way we use .htm files for web pages, .doc files for word processing and .xls files for spreadsheets, GEDCOM files (they usually end in .ged) are used for genealogical research. Most big-name genealogical research software supports the GEDCOM format. For example, Heritage Family Tree Deluxe can both create and import GEDCOM files. That means you can access the LDS Church's data for your research, and also add your own findings to fill in any gaps in the available databases.

To download a GEDCOM file, you need to do two things. First of all, you need to find an appropriate family tree by using the search feature on RootsWeb to find your ancestors; secondly, you need to find a downloadable GEDCOM file associated with those individuals. Not all family trees come with GEDCOM files; it's up to the submitter to specify whether or not their research can be downloaded. In most cases, though, if the information is in RootsWeb then there's a GEDCOM file to go with it.

Using our example of the missionary Judd, we can look at his record on RootsWeb to find a number of links above his details:

- Index shows where that individual sits in their family tree.
- Descendancy shows their direct descendants (if any).
- Register shows a short summary of the individual's birth, death and descendants.
- Pedigree shows their parents and grandparents in a similar view to the one we've already used in Heritage Family Tree Deluxe.
- Ahnentafel does roughly the same thing in a different layout (Ahnentafel is German for 'ancestor table').
- Download GEDCOM enables you to download the data file and import it into your family tree software. We'll come back to that in a moment.
- Post-Em notes are the electronic equivalent of Post-It notes.

Playing with Post-Ems

Even the most diligent researcher can make mistakes, and sometimes information – particularly information about long-lost ancestors – can be sketchy, contradictory or very basic. You might find that a researcher has incorrect information which you can correct, or you might be able to shed light on an individual about whom the researcher hasn't been able to dig up much information. You'd use Post-Em notes for both of these things.

In addition to the biographical information for individuals, RootsWeb lets you view family tree data in a variety of ways and download the data for use in your family tree software.

Taylor & Hudson; Dyer & Tarn

Entries: 490   Updated: 2005-02-09 04:58:37 UTC (Wed)   Contact: Brian York   *brian@seasonalspecialties.com*

Index | Descendancy | Register | Pedigree | Ahnentafel | Download GEDCOM | Add Post-em

- *ID:* 1274
- *Name:* "Zhu Mingyang" Charles Henry JUDD
- *Sex:* M
- *Birth:* BEF 26 JUL 1842 in Loughborough, Leicestershire, England [1]
- *Note:*

> Charles Henry Judd, British missionary (male), was christened at All Saints, Loughborough, Leicestershire, England, on 26 July 1842, the son of Robert Judd and (Mrs.) Jane Judd.
> Originally a bank clerk from Loughborough, he became a student at the Church Missionary Training College at Islington, London, preparing to join the CMS. However, he felt uncomfortable with infant baptism. He had attended meetings at Welbeck Street and knew the CMS missionary Frederick Gough. After the Lammermuir party had sailed for China, Judd became aware of the writings of Grattan Guinness, and at Gough's home in Bow, east London, met Thomas J. Barnardo. As a consequence, he became aware of J. Hudson Taylor's mission and left the CMS training institute. For about one year he lived with W. T. Berger at Saint Hill, near East Grinstead, Sussex, as a tutor in English.
> Having married in October 1867, Judd left for China with Mrs. Ann Bohannan, the Cardwells, and Edward Fishe. The party arrived in China on 3 March 1868.

You can attach a Post-Em to any individual's data in the RootsWeb database by clicking on the Add Post-Em link. You'll be asked for your name and email address, and you can also specify a web page address – for example, the address of the page of your site providing the necessary information. You can then add a note, which the original researcher can read. Finally, you need to choose a password. This password enables you to edit your Post-Em note at a later date, and it means that only you can change or delete the note.

As you'd expect, other people can leave Post-Ems for you: if you've uploaded your family tree research, don't be surprised if you receive Post-Ems from other people who've spotted an error or who can fill in the blanks in your research. It's an excellent system and works very well.

You can use RootsWeb's Post-Em notes to notify researchers of additional information or of errors, and other people can do the same with your data.

RootsWeb.com
The oldest and largest FREE genealogy site, supported by Ancestry.com

Home | Searches | Family Trees | Mailing Lists | Message Boards | Web Sites | Passwords | Help

Post-em Interactive Edit

Return to WorldConnect

Database: :3053414
Individual: 1274

Your Name		(required)
Your Email		(required)

If you'd like to link to a page with additional information, enter the page reference before (optional)

URL	
URL Title	

Note (required)	

Password	(Required)

(Preview) (Post)

PART  Importing a GEDCOM file

When you've found a branch of your family tree, you can download all the relevant data in GEDCOM format. You can do this in two ways: you can download the entire GEDCOM file for that individual, which means you'll also get branches of their family tree that have little or no connection with your own ancestors, or you can specify the GEDCOM data you'd like to download. If you go for this latter option you can specify whether you want to download information about an individual's ancestors or their descendants, and you can specify the number of generations that should be included. By default, the options are set to ancestors for 10 generations.

Once you've downloaded the file, you can import it into Heritage Family Tree Deluxe by choosing File > Import. We'd recommend creating a brand new family tree database in the program first: that way you can see whether the data is appropriate to your research without committing it to your master database just yet. To do this, use the following steps;

Launch Heritage Family Tree Deluxe (if it isn't already running) and click File > New. We're going to create a new, blank project to see what information we can get from the GEDCOM file we've downloaded, so give the project a meaningful name such as 'test database for gedcom data'. Click Create when you've done this.

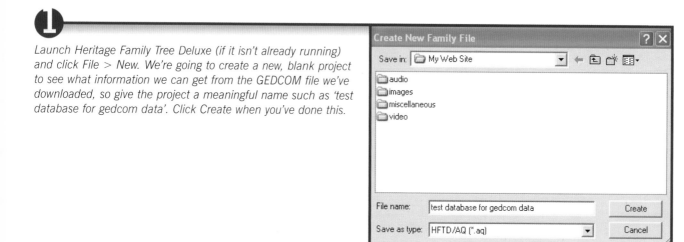

You should now see a completely blank family tree. Time to add some data. Click File > Import and navigate to the folder where you saved your downloaded GEDCOM data; we saved it to the desktop, as you can see in this screenshot. Click Open to continue.

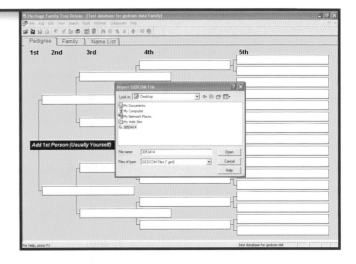

Heritage Family Tree Deluxe will now ask you what information you want to import. As we're experimenting, let's see what happens if we tick every button in the dialog box. Click the OK button to continue.

This screen asks you to cite your sources: it's considered polite to acknowledge others' hard work. However, for now we'll just skip this screen so we can see what information is actually in the GEDCOM file. Click the OK button to continue.

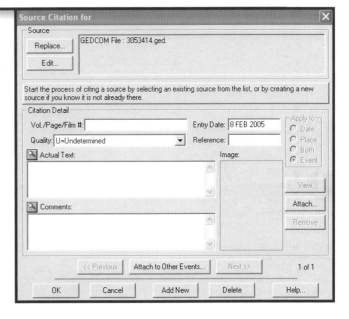

After a few seconds, you should see a dialog box something like this, telling you that the import process has been successful. In this example we've successfully added details of five individuals and two marriages to our database.

Once again we're back in the familiar Pedigree view, and as you can see Heritage Family Tree Deluxe has added people's information in exactly the same way as if we'd typed it ourselves. You can navigate around the family tree by clicking on people's names; click the Family tab to see their full details.

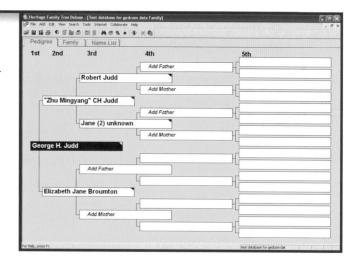

Click the Edit menu and choose Edit Individual. This brings up the key information about that individual, and as you can see everything has been stored in the correct place. The GEDCOM file can also contain notes; to see them, click the Notes/Sources button.

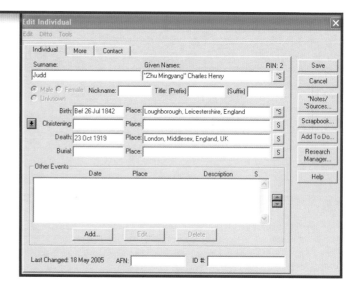

And here's the Notes view for Charles Judd the missionary. If you click the Individual Sources tab you'll see the researcher's notes on where he or she found the information; Marriage Notes will show you details of the individual's marriage (where appropriate), and Marriage Sources will show the source of that information.

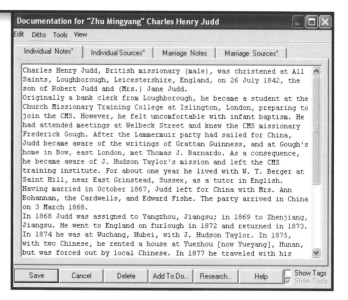

PART 8 Sharing your research the GEDCOM way

As we've already seen, the world of genealogical research is based on the principle of share and share alike so, when you've completed your research, it's a very good idea to share it with others – particularly if you've benefited from other people's efforts. To do this it's just a matter of creating your GEDCOM file and uploading it to the RootsWeb site.

GEDCOM file formats
But before you can do that you need to know the different kinds of files you can create. Heritage Family Tree Deluxe can produce four kinds of GEDCOM file:

Standard
Use this kind of file if you want to share your GEDCOM data with people who don't necessarily use Heritage Family Tree Deluxe.

Standard w/HTFD Enh.
This stands for 'with Heritage Family Tree Deluxe Enhancements', and it provides more data than the standard GEDCOM format. Only use this format if you're 100% certain that everybody who will use the file has a copy of Heritage Family Tree Deluxe; it's best suited to swapping information with fellow researchers than for uploading data to the internet.

Ancestral File
This format is for submitting data to the Ancestral File database, a slightly different project to the main RootsWeb database.

Temple Names
Again, this format is for a slightly different database called TempleReady.

Creating a GEDCOM file from your research
In this short workshop, we'll turn our Heritage Family Tree Deluxe data into a working GEDCOM file.

Open Heritage Family Tree Deluxe and open your research project (the real one, not the dummy one we created in our last workshop). From the File Menu, choose Export; you should now see a dialog box that looks like the one in our screenshot.

By default, Heritage Family Tree Deluxe exports in the Standard w/HFTD Enh. Format. You'll need to change this to Standard format for uploading data to RootsWeb. To do this, click Standard in the Export Type section. Make sure that in the Selected Individuals section at the bottom of the dialog box, the 'All' option is ticked.

Click Export and give your GEDCOM file a name. It's a good idea to export the file to your desktop so that you can find it again, although you can of course store it in any folder you like. Click the Export button to start building the file.

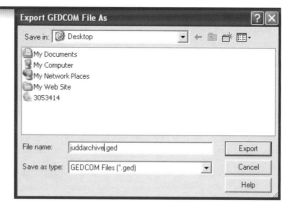

Heritage Family Tree Deluxe will now begin to export the GEDCOM data. Don't worry if this dialog box appears on screen for a while; the export process isn't very quick and, if you've got a very big database, it's probably a good idea to make yourself a cup of tea.

Eventually you should see a dialog box that looks like this one. This means that the export process has completed successfully; click OK to return to Heritage Family Tree Deluxe. You can close the program now; for the next workshop, all you'll need is your web browser.

Uploading your data to RootsWeb

In this final workshop we'll discover how you can upload your GEDCOM data to the RootsWeb site. This means your research will be available to the whole world. It's very important that your research is as exhaustive as possible before you do this; the more information you can give others, the more benefit they'll get from your research.

Launch your web browser and head to the RootsWeb site at **www.rootsweb.com**. Scroll down the page and you'll see a section headed 'Family Trees (WorldConnect)'; in this section you should see a link marked 'Submit your family tree'. Click this link to continue.

You need to create a User Code – a user name – and a password before you can continue. You'll use this code and password to log in to RootsWeb in the future, and you won't be able to upload, edit or delete your GEDCOM file without them. Choose your code and password and then click the Standard button to continue.

If your choice of user name hasn't already been taken, you'll now be asked for your name and your email address. Enter the information and then click the Setup button to continue; use the Oops button to go back and correct any mistakes.

After a few seconds you'll see the User Setup/Edit screen as per our screenshot. The name, email address and password should already be filled in. In the Display options section, enter a name for your database and then specify whether surnames should be printed in uppercase letters.

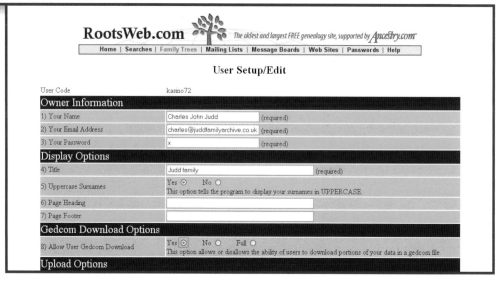

Scroll down and you'll see the Upload Options shown here. In the first field, use the Browse button to locate the GEDCOM file you created in the last workshop. If you wish, you can change the other options on this screen (for now, we'll leave them as they are). Click Upload/Update to continue.

If you thought it took a while to create your GEDCOM file, uploading it takes even longer: we'd definitely recommend putting the kettle on or going on holiday. Eventually, though, the file will be uploaded and you'll see the confirmation page shown here.

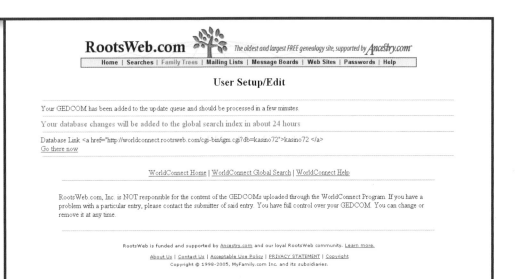

If you click the Go There Now link you'll be able to see your family tree information; click a letter to see all of the entries for that letter (in this screenshot we've used J for Judd) and then on a name to see the entries for that name.

Protecting people's privacy

While many of the people in your family tree will be deceased, you will probably include plenty of relatives who are still alive and well: your parents, for example, or distant cousins. Although of course no family tree would be complete without details of your living relatives, you need to strike an important balance between providing full details and protecting people's privacy. For example, would Uncle Ed be happy if he discovered that his turbulent marriage history was freely available on the internet for anyone to read? Would another relative be chuffed if people could look them up on the net and discover that nobody knows who their father was? Privacy is important – not just to protect others, but to protect yourself from irate relatives!

Whether you're publishing your family information on your own website or via the RootsWeb site, it's important to think carefully

about your living relatives before uploading any data. If there are any skeletons in your family's cupboard, is it a good idea to include their details in your GEDCOM file? Would your relatives be more comfortable if you didn't include their first names?

The RootsWeb site has its own solution to the problem: unless you specify otherwise, the records of anyone in your GEDCOM file born after 1930 and still living will be changed: instead of a first name and surname, they'll be listed as 'Judd [Living]'. You can also choose to remove source data or notes from the records of living people, or remove records altogether. As you'll see on RootsWeb's Frequently Asked Questions page (**http://helpdesk.rootsweb.com/FAQ/wcsubmit8.html**), you can remove entire groups of people at once. For example, it's possible to remove person X and all of his or her descendants in one fell swoop.

INTERNET GENEALOGY MANUAL

PART 9 Appendices

PART  9

Appendix 1 – Working with digital audio

We've mentioned the possibility of interviewing family members, particularly elderly relatives with their invaluable and irreplaceable knowledge of who is, and was, who. There are four basic approaches to conducting an interview:

- Asking questions and receiving answers in writing, either via letters or email.
- Having a chat face-to-face or on the telephone, making notes and transcribing information manually.
- Recording an interview.
- Filming an interview.

You can, of course, mix and match these approaches, perhaps presenting the bulk of the information as a transcript but including a short video clip of a particularly pertinent point of the interview.

We'll look at video in the following appendix. First, though, a word on working with audio.

Testing, testing

If you have the appropriate equipment to hand, you can record your interview directly onto a digital recorder. For instance, many MP3 music players are equipped with microphone sockets and can record audio directly to an internal hard disk or memory card. The recording can then be transferred to your PC. If it's already in a suitable file format, such as MP3, you can perform any required editing and easily publish the file in your online family archive. Failing that, you may have to convert the file format first. We recommend that you should use the MP3 format for maximum compatibility. You want anybody who visits your

An old analogue tape recorder is fine for interviews but the trick is turning your recording into a digital file for your family archive.

If you record digitally, you can transfer the recording directly to your computer.

website to be able to enjoy the recording, and just about every computer can play MP3 files. MP3 files are also reasonably small, panning out at about 500KB to 1MB per minute, depending on your chosen quality settings. If your recording device has the option, set it to record in MP3 format.

If you don't have a portable digital recorder, you could connect a microphone to the computer and record your interview directly onto the computer's hard disk. This rather assumes that your subject pays you a home visit, although if you have a laptop you have greater flexibility to take it with you when you travel for a chat.

However, there's every possibility that you have only a traditional cassette recorder. This is absolutely fine for recording granny or grandad but there is one rather obvious problem: how do you get the recording from the cassette to your website? The answer is to transfer it first to your computer. But that merely raises another dilemma: how do you connect a cassette recorder to a computer?

Here's how.

Making connections

First, consider your computer. If it has speakers, it has a sound card. This is an internal component that produces sound for playback through speakers or headphones. And if it has a sound card, it can almost certainly record sound, too. Have a look around next to the speaker connections for a small (3.5mm) jack labelled 'line-in' or 'mic-in'. As these names (almost) suggest, the mic-in jack provides a connection for a microphone and the line-in jack provides a connection for any other type of device, including a cassette recorder. You may find that you have both. However, the inputs may not be labelled at all or may be flagged with indecipherable symbols, in which case consult the manual that came with your computer.

If your computer has no sound capability, now might be the time to upgrade it. You can install an internal sound card very easily. However, for an even simpler life, invest in an external sound card. This is a device that connects to a computer via USB and provides all the circuitry and sockets found in a standard sound card. The 510EX from Trust (**www.trust.com**) costs around £30.

Let's assume that your computer has a sound card and that you manage to track down its line-in or mic-in jack, or indeed both. All you have to do now is connect your cassette recorder to the computer. Quite how you do this depends on the following:

If your cassette recorder has a pair of chunky phono outputs – one for the left channel; one for the right – you can connect these outputs directly to the sound card's line-in input. You'll need a cable with a single stereo 3.5mm jack on one end and two phono plugs on the other (or an adapter that converts one type of cable to the other).

If your cassette recorder has a headphone socket, you can connect this to the sound card instead. As the headphone socket will probably use the $1/4$-inch standard, you'll need a cable with a

An external sound card is easier than an internal upgrade.

This cable has a 3.5mm stereo plug on one end and phono plugs on the other.

stereo 3.5mm plug on the sound card end and a $1/4$-inch plug on the other, or an adapter. In this scenario, you should use the sound card's mic-in socket rather than the line-in (given a choice), as the mic-in socket provides helpful additional amplification.

If your cassette recorder has a 3.5mm output, connect this to the sound card using a standard cable with 3.5mm plugs on both ends. No conversion is required.

A visit to Maplin or any other high street electronics shop may be in order for the requisite cables.

Software solutions

Copying audio from cassette to computer is easy if you use software designed for the task. One good example is Roxio Creator 7.5 Supersonic (about £53 from **www.roxio.co.uk**); another is Nero 6 Reloaded (about £35 from **www.nero.com**). These are both fully-fledged CD/DVD suites that include modules for capturing analogue audio recordings from tape or vinyl. In fact, you may already have one or the other on your system.

Alternatively, Windows XP users might consider Microsoft Plus! Digital Media Edition. This costs a mere £13 (**www.microsoft.com/windows/plus/PlusHome.asp**) and includes an Analog Recorder utility that's designed specifically to help you record from LP or cassette. However, recordings are saved in the Windows Media Audio (WMA) format which is not quite so universally compatible as MP3 files. Any Windows computer will be able to play your recording when you publish it in your archive but Mac users may have to install their own software first. If you use Analog Recorder, we recommend that you convert your WMA files to MP3 before publishing them. There are many utilities that can handle this. In fact, we discuss a program called dBpowerAmp in the following pages. This can handle WMA-to-MP3 conversion nicely so long as you first download the WMA codec (see **www.dbpoweramp.com/codec-central-wma.htm** for details).

A simple adapter lets you connect a 3.5mm sound card cable to a ?-inch headphone jack.

Plus! Analog Recorder is an easy way to capture audio from a cassette.

Capturing a recording from cassette

In the following workshop, we'll use Wave Editor, a module
included with Nero Reloaded. As always, you can achieve the
same results with any similar software. Begin by connecting the
cassette player to the computer using one of the cable/adapter
suggestions above.

*First, check your PC's recording setup. In Windows XP, open the
Control Panel from the Start menu, click Sounds, Speech, and
Audio Devices, and then click 'Adjust the system volume'. Open
the Audio tab in the Sound and Audio Device Properties dialogue
screen. (To get to the same place in Windows Me, double-click
the Sounds and Multimedia icon in the Control Panel and open
the Audio tab.) Check that your sound card appears as the
default device in the 'Sound recording' field and click the
Volume button.*

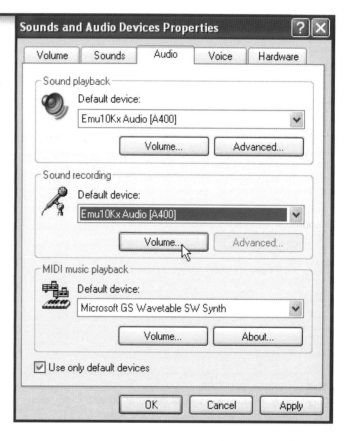

*In the Recording Control window, ensure that the appropriate
recording input is active. If your cassette recorder is connected
to the line-in socket, the preferred option, put a check mark in
the Line-In box and set the slider at about the halfway point; if it
is connected to the microphone socket, check and adjust the
Microphone controls instead. Note that in earlier versions of
Windows you'll find a Mute box below each slider, which
effectively turns that input off.*

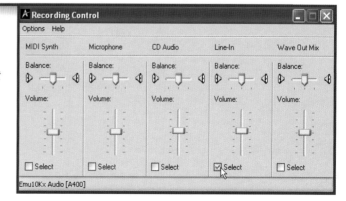

3

What happens now varies according to your choice of software but you should always start by establishing two all-important criteria: the recording quality and the volume level. Start playing your tape in the cassette recorder and you should hear the sound through your computer speakers (or headphones). Now start Nero Wave Editor, click the Audio toolbar button, and select 'Record'.

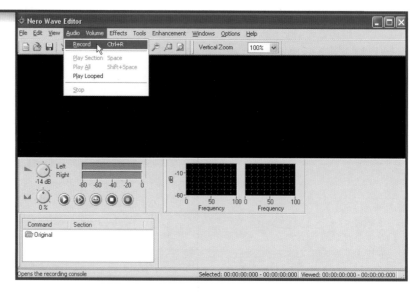

4

By default, Wave Editor records at CD-quality level. There's no point going for a higher quality setting, as the cassette source simply doesn't warrant it, but nor should you sacrifice quality by selecting a lower setting unless hard disk space is at an absolute premium. Click OK to proceed.

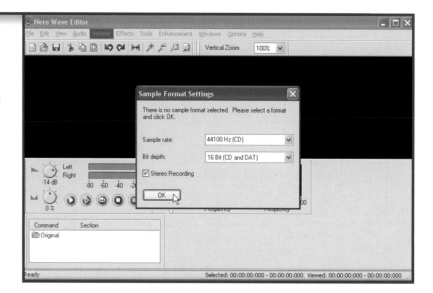

5

If possible, play the loudest part of the recording – a spot of laughter, perhaps – and watch the Recording Console's Input Level meters carefully. If they hit the top (0dB), your recording will be distorted; but if they hover around the lower sections throughout, your recording may be too quiet. If necessary, return to the Windows Recording Control screen (step 2 above) and reposition the line-in (or mic) slider. Keep an eye on the Wave Editor meters and settle on a position where the loudest parts of the recording approach but do not quite reach the 0dB mark.

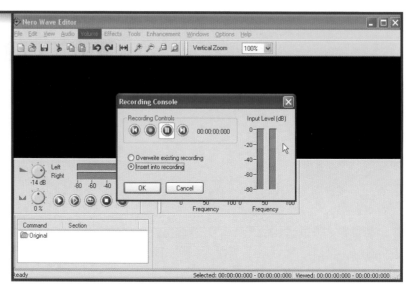

Now prepare your cassette to play from the beginning and click the red record button in the Recording Console. Start playing the tape immediately. Don't worry about capturing a few seconds of silence at the start, as this can be easily removed later. Capture the entire recording in one go, even if it's full of gaps and bits you know that you won't want to keep.

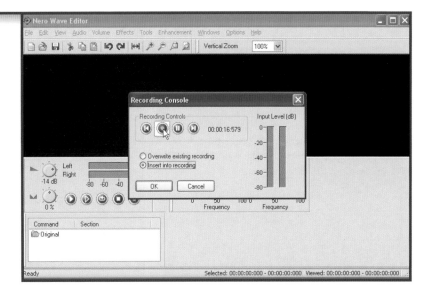

When the recording is finished, click OK in Wave Editor's Recording Console to stop the transfer. You must now save the captured file to the computer's hard disk. Click File, then Save, and save the file (with a meaningful name) in the folder of your choice. That's it: you now have a single digital audio file in WAV format.

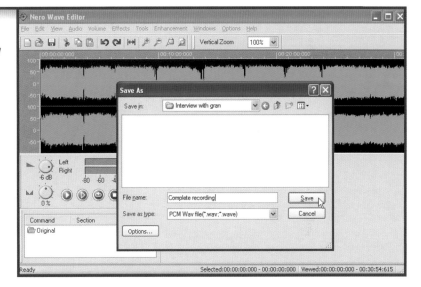

It's time for an edit. Click anywhere in the waveform – this is a graphical representation of the recording – and drag the cursor to the right while holding down the mouse button. This selects a portion of the file. Now click the Play button, and you'll hear that segment of the recording. Experiment until you manage to roughly select part of the recording that you definitely want to keep.

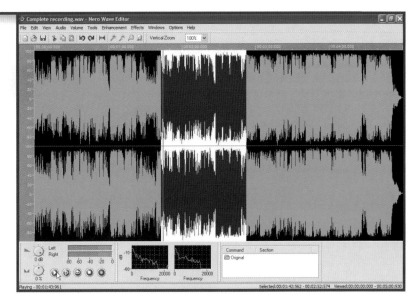

Now click the Edit menu and select 'Copy to File'. This isolates the selected part of the recording and saves it as a unique file. Choose a destination folder and ensure that WAV remains the selected file format. Don't worry if your selection starts before the bit you want or ends after it; the important thing here is NOT to miss the beginning or the end.

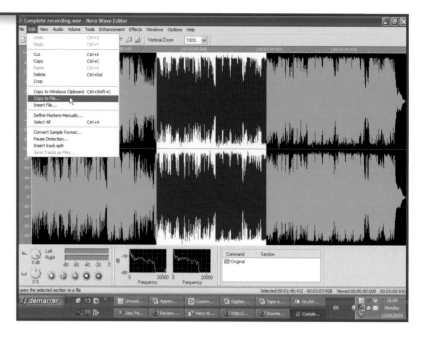

Open the file you've just saved in Wave Editor and trim any surplus material fore and aft until you end up with just the part of the recording that you want to keep. To do this, repeat Step 8 but concentrate on starting and finishing the selection at just the right points. (There are in fact several ways to trim a track in Wave Editor but this method is as good as any.) Save this selection as another unique file. You should now have three files in your folder: the original recording, the first rough edit (Step 9), and the final edit (this step). Repeat Steps 8 and 9 as often as necessary until you have isolated and saved each segment of the original recording that you want to keep.

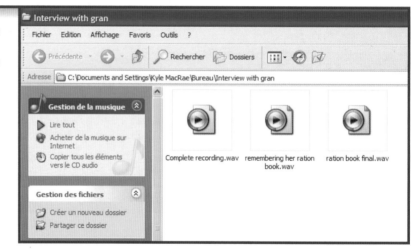

All that remains is to convert your saved files to the MP3 file format. For this, forget Wave Editor and turn instead to one of the many free converters. Here we'll use dBpowerAmp Music Converter (free for 30 days from **www.dbpoweramp.com/dmc.htm**). Download and install dBpowerAmp, then launch the program and select one of your final WAV files. Select MP3 in the conversion format field.

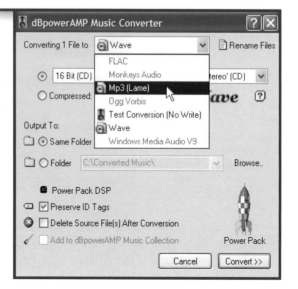

Adjust the slider to select an MP3 quality level. The further to the left you move the slider, the lower the quality but also the smaller the file size. File sizes are important on the internet; the smaller a file, the quicker it downloads and so the sooner a recording can be heard. Experiment here, but a bit rate of 128 or 112Kbps should suffice. For a long recording of more than 3 or 4 minutes, see if you can get away with 96Kbps. Bear in mind that the quality of the original tape recording may not be fantastic and you can't improve on that here.

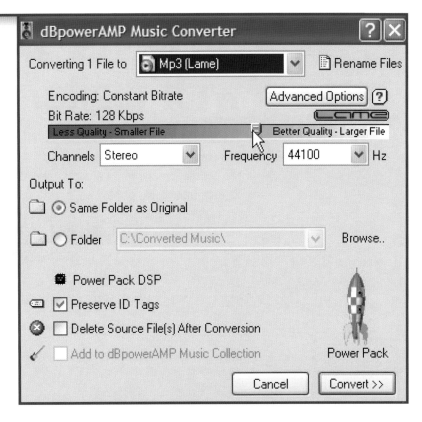

Click Convert and let dBpowerAmp do its stuff. The result will be an MP3 file that's around one-tenth (in terms of file size, not length!) of the original WAV file. Repeat with your other saved files. You can now add your MP3 files to your family archive, either within scrapbooks (see p150) or linked directly from the archive's front page.

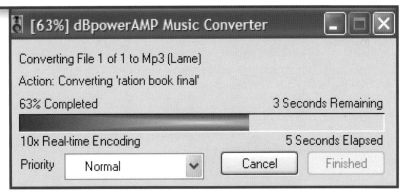

It's worth pointing out that Wave Editor and similar programs come stacked with tools that can help you improve the quality of analogue recordings. You might, for instance, be able to reduce or even remove tape hiss. Play around with the options. However, don't get too hung up on any of this. Your aim is simply to bring your family archive to life with a recording of somebody dear reminiscing about the old days.

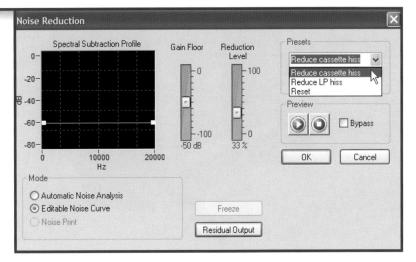

PART

Appendix 2 – Working with digital video

Just as you can include audio clips in your archive, so you can have video. Nothing brings a family tree to life like a little footage of an elderly relative reminiscing while looking though old photographs, or a grandchild filmed on a grandparent's knee. But we'll leave the creative side of things to you. Here's an overview of the technicalities.

Go digital

Actually, there's only one real technical issue and that concerns your camcorder. If you have an older analogue camcorder – VHS or Hi-8 or similar – then you have a problem when it comes to transferring footage to your computer. You'll need either an internal video capture card or an external gadget that lets you hook up your camcorder and perform an analogue-to-digital conversion. This is possible, but it's a bind and far more hassle than working with an analogue cassette recorder.

To our minds, digital is unequivocally the way to go. All digital camcorders have FireWire sockets, and FireWire is the interface of choice for shifting video files from camcorder to computer. Just connect the camcorder to the computer with a cable and away you go (as we shall see in a moment). If your PC doesn't have a FireWire socket, you can upgrade it easily with a FireWire expansion card.

With FireWire, you can connect a digital camcorder to your computer and transfer footage in a flash (well, in real time, at least).

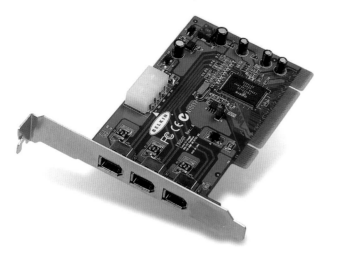

A FireWire expansion card is cheap and easy to install.

Capturing footage

Before you can publish a video clip on the web, you must transfer raw video footage from your camcorder's tape to the computer's hard drive and produce an edited movie. This process is called capturing and it requires specialist software. However, if you use Windows XP, you already have a suitable tool to hand in the form of Windows Movie Maker. Here's an overview of how to capture, edit and produce a movie with Movie Maker.

One important note. To get the best out of Movie Maker, a free upgrade from version 1 to version 2 is essential. However, Microsoft has seen fit to withdraw this as a standalone download option and Movie Maker 2 is now only available bundled with Windows XP Service Pack 2.

Connect your digital camcorder to your computer via a FireWire cable and switch it to playback mode. Open Movie Maker 2, expand the Capture Video section and click Capture from video device. You should now be able to select your camcorder as the source device. You'll be asked to name your project.

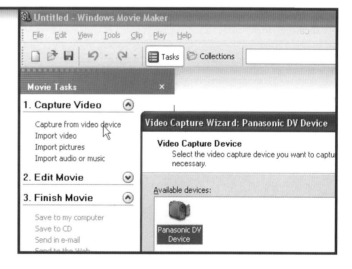

Here you must select a capture setting. Disk space permitting – you'll need around 1GB per five minutes of footage – we strongly suggest that you go for the DV-AVI option, as this captures video at its native quality without applying any upfront compression. It's better to leave compression until the end (see Step 9).

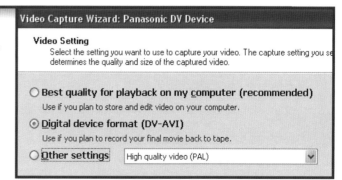

3

The next couple of screens are self-explanatory – you can choose whether to work manually or automatically and ask Movie Maker to detect or ignore scene changes – and eventually the program will rewind the camcorder tape and capture the video.

4

Assuming you asked Movie Maker to detect scene changes, you will end up with an array of consecutive clips in the main program window. Movie Maker calls this a collection. You can now import additional elements into your collection, such as still images and music files.

5

Drag and drop clips into the storyboard and reorder them to suit. In the Edit Movie sidebar, you'll find Movie Maker's tools for trimming clips, applying special effects, adding scene transitions – as shown here – and more.

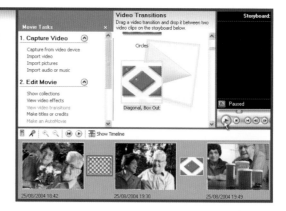

6

Switch to the timeline view to include a soundtrack or if you want fuller control over your clips. For instance, if you imported an MP3 track into your collection earlier, you can drag it from the collection directly into the audio track and determine its start point and duration. This can add atmosphere to a clip. However, it also means that your video file will be substantially larger and thus slower to download and play.

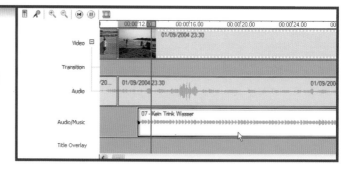

7

You can also enhance your movie with titles and captions. Type your text and tell Movie Maker whether you want to add an opening title page, end credits or a caption to accompany any clip. Drag the edited title into the Title Overlay track if you wish to superimpose text on a clip or image.

8

Movie Maker's editing tools are straightforward and fun and you should be able to produce a pretty proficient movie project. But you will not as yet have made an actual video. For this, access the program's Finish Movie controls. Click Save to my computer and, in the next screen, give your video file a name.

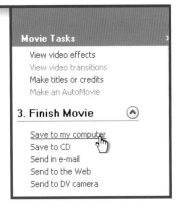

9

The vital bit: check the Other settings option and make a choice. You should experiment a little here. If you choose one of the broadband settings, the video quality will be better but the file will be bigger; if you go for the dial-up option, you'll sacrifice playback quality but end up with a much smaller file that will load and play more quickly when it's in your online archive. Try a couple of options. You can save your movie as often as you like in different configurations.

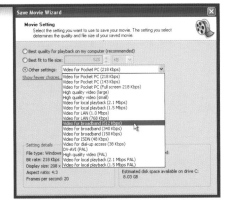

10

When Movie Maker has finished saving the file, play it in Windows Media Player. This is what your visitors will see when you publish the video in your family archive website. If the frame size is too small, as here (this video was saved in the dial-up setting), try one of the higher quality settings. What'll you'll end up with is a video file with a WMV extension. Now just pop it in a scrapbook in your archive, as described on p150.

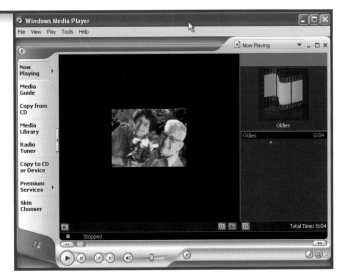

Index

Author acknowledgements:
Grateful thanks to Jill MacRae and Gary Marshall

Author	**Kyle MacRae**
Copy Editor	**Shena Deuchars**
Front cover family tree	**Marie Lynskey**
Page build	**James Robertson**
Index	**Nigel d'Auvergne**
Project Manager	**Louise McIntyre**